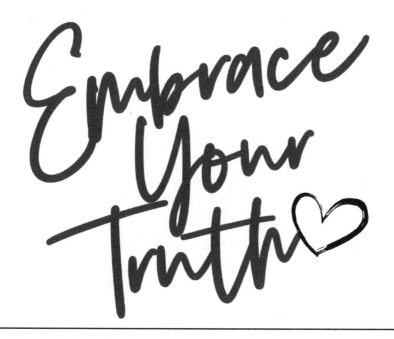

Embrace Your Truth

A Journey of Authenticity

GABRIELLE CLAIBORNE
WITH LINDA TATRO HERZER

TRANSFORMATION
JOURNEYS WORLDWIDE

Published by
Transformation Journeys Worldwide
Atlanta, Georgia

Special discounts available on quantity purchases by corporations and associations. Contact the "Special Sales Department" at info@TransformationJourneysWW.com for details.

Embrace Your Truth: A Journey of Authenticity/Gabrielle Claiborne with Linda Tatro Herzer
ISBN: 978-1-7351974-0-1

While the author has made every effort to provide accurate Internet addresses and other contact information at the time of this publication, neither the publisher nor the author assumes any responsibility for errors or for changes that ocur after publication. Further, the publisher does not have any control over and does not assume any responsibility for author or third-party websites or their content.

To the first person I ever came out to, whose support and acceptance allowed me to step into a world that I never imagined possible, and . . .

To each reader who is longing to embrace some aspect of your truth—whatever that looks like for you—and is looking for ways to overcome the fears that so easily keep us stuck. May you find support for your journey here.

CONTENTS

At one time or another, each of us confronts an experience so powerful, bewildering, joyous, or terrifying that all our efforts to see it as a "problem" are futile. Each of us is brought to the cliff's edge. At such moments we can either back away in bitterness or confusion, or leap forward into mystery. And what does mystery ask of us? Only that we be in its presence, that we fully, consciously, hand ourselves over. That is all, and that is everything.

—Phillip Simmons, *Learning to Fall*

Introduction

"Have you chosen a name for yourself?"

That was the question posed to me by Ramona, my midwife and mentor, who helped me—a person who had been raised as a male—give birth to my true feminine self.

For the first forty-nine years of my life, I never dared dream I could actually be called by a feminine name—even though I had always felt an attraction to feminine things and had secretly dressed in women's clothes since childhood. But Ramona's question opened that door and started me on a quest for a name that expressed the truth of my being.

While some transgender people choose the masculine or feminine equivalent of their given name—Danielle for Daniel, Patrick for Patricia—I decided not to go that route, but to keep only my initials: GEC. Because my personal relationship with God has always been vital to me, I began looking online for a

Hebrew name, knowing that Hebrew was the original language of the Old Testament. In searching in the "Gs" under girl names, I came across *Gabrielle* and learned it means "strength of God." A search under the "Es" brought me to *Elena*—"light of God." Ramona was the one who suggested the last name of *Claiborne*. Since I admired Liz Claiborne's fashion designs, I went with it.

In the Bible, and in many cultures, a person's name reveals who they are. In choosing the name *Gabrielle Elena Claiborne*, I was seeking to reveal my deepest—although up until that time, hidden—understanding of and hopes for myself. I wanted to be strong, and I had no doubt that I would need all the strength of God to finally acknowledge the truth I had struggled to suppress for years. I also knew I wanted to be the light of God, to live my life with more purpose and more impact than I had lived it to that point.

In many cultures, the act of naming is also an act of power, with the one doing the naming holding power over the person named. Consequently, choosing a new name was an act of turning away from the power the world had exercised over me by unwittingly burdening me with a masculine name. It was a way to reclaim my own power, the power that comes from living one's truth. In time, I also came to understand it as a decision to be faithful to God by being true to the person God had created me to be.

Throughout our lives, the world has saddled all of us—regardless of who we are—with various names and labels. Some truly reveal our essence; some rob us of our power. I share my story in hopes that it may inspire you to let go of any labels that obscure the real you, so you can reclaim your power. May it be an invitation for you to embrace all the brilliant facets of your truth—no matter what those are for you.

I recognize that no single person's journey can serve as a comprehensive, one-size-fits-all guide for how to live your life authentically. That is why I offer my story as an invitation—not a "how to" manual. I also recognize that if you do not identify as transgender or gender diverse, then you may think you have little in common with me—which might be true. But several years into my gender transition I realized that, in order to step into our authenticity, the things *all people* have to work through are basically the same—whether we are transgender or not.

This led me to share my story through a personal growth workshop. I enlisted the assistance of a cisgender minister (*cisgender* describes people who identify with the gender they were assigned at birth, the opposite of *transgender*) to help me create and co-present the workshop. Throughout the interactive event, attendees were invited to engage in exercises that would help them apply, to their own lives, the lessons I had learned on my journey. Because all the participants (and most of them were cisgender) found these exercises helpful, I have included some of them at the end of each chapter, under the heading "Your Turn." Give them a try if you would like to jump-start your own journey to authenticity. To find more support for your journey, consider reading the authors listed at the end of this book, whose wisdom I quote and reference throughout these chapters.

To highlight the areas of work in which we must all engage in order to embrace our truths, I have arranged my story in thematic, rather than chronological, order. To get a sneak peek at these universal themes, keep reading. If you like to arrive at the theater fifteen minutes late so you can miss the previews and get right to the movie, skip the next section of this introduction and jump to chapter 1. If you have little knowledge of the trans experience, consider reading the appendix, "Understanding Transgender People," now. And if you come across unfamiliar trans-related words, see the glossary for terms and definitions. Regardless of the order in which you choose to continue, my hope is that the story you find here will give you the courage to embrace all the facets of *your* truth. May you discover, as I have, not a life without challenges, but one of joyous peace, life-giving power, and world-changing purpose.

Previews of Coming Attractions

The journey of embracing your truth begins with listening to your heart. But how exactly do you do that? In chapter 1, you will discover the languages through which your heart speaks—your attractions, feelings, intuitions, dreams, and bodily symptoms. You will learn about these languages from a negative example, as I share how I ignored my heart's voice for four decades, even though it was speaking to me through each of these five different languages.

As you embark on your journey to greater authenticity, creating a support system can be highly beneficial. In chapter 2, I tell you about the wonderful individuals, authors, and groups without whom I literally would not have survived the early years of my gender transition.

In chapter 3, we explore various things you can do to deepen your self-love and self-acceptance. You will learn about the life-giving practices of mirror work, letting go of limiting beliefs, reprogramming your old, negative thoughts with positive affirmations, and the importance of not just listening to your heart, but acting on what it says.

Part of letting go of limiting beliefs involves reframing your past and coming to see it in a more positive light—especially if it involves many failures or things you are ashamed of, as mine did. This is the topic we explore in chapter 4, along with how to ignore the abusive voice of our inner critic. I also share how I learned to do something very difficult, but incredibly life-giving: forgive others *and*—what was even harder—forgive myself.

Embracing our truths inevitably involves making changes—changes that may impact the lives of those closest to us—changes they may not want and may not welcome. This means we have to prepare for pushback. In chapter 5, we consider whether we need to step away from those from whom we receive the greatest pushback—at least temporarily—or if we can choose to hold space for our loved ones as they navigate the impact our changes are having on them. You will hear how I came to respond to the accusation that I was being selfish, and also learn how I was able to do one of the most difficult things I have ever done: let go of guilt.

In chapter 6, we shift our focus from the *things we must do* to embrace our truth, to *how we want to live* once we step into our authenticity. I invite you to live inside out, to embrace your truth fiercely and live it courageously, regardless of what others say or think. You will learn how I pumped up the volume of my truth through a life coach who taught me to connect with my feelings. I also encourage you to experiment with various ways to amplify *your* authenticity: journaling, sharing on social media, spending time in your favorite setting, and just doing the things you love.

I firmly believe that embracing our truth leads not only to our own happiness, but to the healing of our world. This happens because authentic living leads to stepping more and more into our purpose. In chapter 7, I share how I found my purpose and began living it . . . not with a full-blown plan in mind, but by just starting somewhere and being willing to play in bigger arenas as opportunities arose. You also hear how the wisdom of author, speaker, and researcher Brené Brown enabled me to rise strong after finding myself face down in one of those arenas. The chapter ends with us considering how we may need to make space in our lives to welcome beneficial things by letting go of what no longer serves us.

Finally, in the epilogue I discuss how the U.S. trans landscape has changed in the last decade. I also share my latest lesson, the one I am still in the midst of learning. It turns out that even after taking a huge step to embrace my truth—as I did when I embraced my gender identity—there is still more to come. I am finding that embracing our truth is a journey more than a destination, an ongoing invitation to continually step into our magnificence.

I look forward to taking this journey with you. Let's begin!

ONE

Listen to Your Heart

"Gabrielle, you're so courageous! I could never do what you did."

This is a comment I often get from audience members who come up and speak to me after hearing my transition story during a training or keynote. To this, I respond with gratitude, a question, and an invitation.

"Thank you. I really appreciate your affirmation. Did you know the word *courage* comes from the Latin word for *heart*? Since we've all got a heart, we all have the capacity for courage. We just have to listen to our hearts and act on what we hear. Believe me, you can be as courageous as I am. You just have to take the first step."

Our Heart's Languages

Listening to my heart was the first step I had to take to embrace my truth—that I am a transgender woman. Sadly, there were many years when I ignored my heart's voice, partly because I did not understand the languages through which it spoke. It wasn't until five years into my gender transition that I read Dr. Paula Reeves' book, *Heart Sense: Unlocking Your Highest Purpose and Deepest Desire*. In this brilliant book, Dr. Reeves explains that our hearts speak through different languages than our heads. While our heads speak in words and thoughts, our hearts communicate through our attractions, feelings, intuitions, dreams, and bodily symptoms or sensations. Once I became aware of the heart's five languages, I realized that, throughout my life, my heart had been speaking to me in all these ways, leading me forward on my journey to authenticity.

Likewise, I recognized that it isn't just me, a transgender woman, who has to listen to my heart. This is a step *all* of us must take, if we desire to live authentically. As I share my journey, I invite you to listen, beyond my story, for how your own heart has been speaking to you through the languages of your attractions, feelings, intuitions, dreams, and bodily symptoms. I invite you to listen so you too can move forward on the life-changing—world-changing—journey of embracing your truth, in all its fullness.

My Journey—In The Beginning

Around the age of nine, the little boy I was being raised as began having an unusual attraction to feminine things. When my family was out of the house I would be drawn to the clothes in my mom's closet. When I tried them on, I experienced deep feelings of peace and contentment—but for the life of me, I couldn't understand why! On the few occasions I got to hang out with my friend's little sister, I noticed I didn't want to just *play* with her Barbie dolls; I wanted to *be* Barbie. Likewise, I became aware that my fascination with my babysitter's bust line was not like most pubescent boys' testosterone-driven attraction. What I really wanted was for my own body to grow breasts like hers!

At the same time as I was noticing my attraction to all things feminine, I developed the thought that there was something wrong about this—something wrong with me—and that I should never tell anyone about this unusual heart's desire. So I never did share the truth of my being; I hid my attraction from everyone and struggled to deny it even to myself for almost four decades.

Part of the reason for my shame and secrecy was because I grew up in a very conservative environment. I was a PK—a preacher's kid—growing up in the Bible belt in the 1960s. But I wasn't just a preacher's kid; I was a fourth-generation Pentecostal preacher's kid! My daddy and my granddaddy and my great grand-daddies—on both sides of my family—had all been Pentecostal preachers, and I was expected to continue the tradition.

While growing up in this conservative culture kept me from sharing what was going on inside me, it also had its upsides. I was blessed with loving, engaged parents who provided much encouragement and every opportunity for my younger sister and me to excel. I had seven years of piano lessons and was on several recreational sports teams during elementary school. When I entered middle school, I would have been content to keep playing rec level sports, but my mom wouldn't hear of it.

"You need to challenge yourself to improve your skills. I

don't want you to settle for average. You're going out for your school's teams."

Which is what I did—but not without protest. All my friends were staying in the rec league, so that's what I wanted to do too. I was comfortable there; rec league sports were familiar, and I was good at them. But Mom was adamant, so off to tryouts I went. While I certainly wasn't happy about it at the time, I ended up being grateful to my mom for encouraging me, from such a young age, to keep growing and becoming the best I could be, to not settle for something just because it was comfortable. In the years to come, that life lesson would serve me well.

Meanwhile, when I wasn't playing sports, I was enjoying a peaceful, privileged childhood—totally oblivious to the civil rights battles and Vietnam War protests raging throughout the nation. My friends and I spent hours exploring the woods around our homes, playing in the creek, and racing our bikes all over town. Of course, I had my chores. Dad taught me how to mow a lawn and Mom instructed me in how to clean a house—skills I would call upon in the early years of my transition.

The highlight of each sweltering, southern summer was the week spent at my grandparents' farm in Alabama. I still remember the pungent smells and dim corners of their old, red barn. My sister and cousins and I would wear ourselves out jumping in the hay and playing hide and seek. But the best thing was when Granddaddy would come by, lift me up on his tractor or backhoe, and let me pretend I was operating those monster machines. They were my Tonka toys on steroids!

Those special weeks at Grandmother and Granddaddy's also

included time working in the garden, shucking peas and husking corn. We'd get all hot and sweaty, laboring under that scorching Alabama sun, then head into their huge old farmhouse for tall glasses of sweetened ice tea.

The only thing that hit the spot any better than that ice tea was my other grandmother's homemade biscuits. I have fond memories of the days I spent at my Georgia grandparent's home and the contests I'd have with my cousin, Tommy. We'd both end up "fuller than a tick" seeing who could eat more of my grandmother's biscuits, warm from the oven, dripping with butter and sorghum syrup. Mm-mmm! Those were happy days!

My church life and Christian faith were an integral part of this happy childhood. At the age of eight, I was born again when I accepted Jesus as my Lord and Savior. Several years later, I experienced the baptism of the Holy Spirit and received the gift of speaking in tongues. What these experiences meant, in my Pentecostal tradition, is that I had been marked by God as a true believer, a faithful follower of Christ. Growing up as a devout Christian and a PK, I was in church for every special event, every Wednesday night service, and twice on Sundays—for morning and evening worship. Saturdays were spent mowing the church lawn with my dad. I also sang with my family in a church choir quartet and earned the equivalency of Eagle Scout status in the Royal Rangers, a Christian program similar to Boy Scouts. More importantly though, I had a relationship with God that was very meaningful to me; I never wanted to do anything displeasing to God.

That is why, during my teen and early adult years, I did

everything I could to repress my "shameful" feminine attractions. In middle school, along with being very involved in church activities and Royal Rangers, I reveled in sports. I made my school's basketball, football, and track teams, and continued to play recreational baseball. In high school, I became even more of a jock. Lettering in track and football required a huge time commitment during the season and still more time off-season, conditioning to play these demanding sports. But I wasn't just a jock; I also got good grades and sang in my school's ensemble and chorus. Being a good-looking, smart athlete who was also a caring Christian and musically talented made me very popular, and I enjoyed dating several girls throughout my high school and college years. Needless to say, I was very, very busy!

While the thrum of all this busy-ness did much to keep me distracted, it never managed to completely drown out the still, small voice of my heart's desire. Every couple of weeks in high school, or when I came home from college for a weekend, if I was alone in the house, I would still be drawn to my mom's closet. There I would dress in her clothes, or more accurately, in her bra and panties, since by this time, none of my mom's clothes—nor my younger sister's—fit my 6'3" frame. This was the late 1970s and early '80s, when personal computers were just starting to be built, and the World Wide Web was still a decade away. But even if I'd had access to the web, I wouldn't have known what terms to search. Having no words to understand my heart's desires, these forays into my mom's closet were always bittersweet. I would feel peaceful and aligned in the moment, but then be riddled with guilt and shame. My Inner Accuser would go on the attack: "Why can't you resist these attractions? Sure, people think you're this big athlete; you can press 210 pounds. But you're nothing but a weakling, a failure."

In college, I continued to try to silence the voice of my heart. I got even busier, making straight A's and playing intramural sports while rushing through Emory University's premed program in three and a half years. After being wait-listed at medical schools two years in a row, I decided to shift gears and went on to Georgia Tech to study civil engineering. This decision was influenced greatly by the high school summers I had spent working in my dad's construction company. My father was what is known as a "tentmaker minister," which means he had a full-time job in addition to pastoring a church. All the time I was growing up, my dad was either the vice president of a large construction company or he owned his own company. Yet, with everything he was doing, he still found time to go to all my games and take me hiking and camping. Dad and I had a great relationship. Since I looked up to him and appreciated the good living he provided for our family, I worked with him the two years I was trying to get into med school and then decided to follow in his vocational footsteps.

While I was still at Georgia Tech, I met and married the smart, beautiful, devout woman of my dreams. Life got even busier during the next seven years as we had three children, each of whom expressed their own unique gifts and talents from very early ages. I loved taking my kids to their sporting events, practices, and recitals and watching them excel as they developed their natural aptitudes. Meanwhile, I moved on from my father's construction company in order to start my own. This eventually led to a successful career in the construction industry and a very nice six-figure income. And on every Sunday morning our family could be found at the large, prestigious Atlanta church where I served as an elder, led a men's Bible study, and sang—sometimes even soloing—in our world-class choir.

By all outward appearances, I had it all. But on the inside, I was living a life of turmoil. More and more I wanted to engage in activities that I perceived to be feminine. As my two daughters got older, I watched with envy as they and my wife left to go get their nails done. I fervently wished I could join them for their shopping sprees and spa days. In fact, my longing to do the things the girls in my family did was so deep that once I actually showed up at a bridal shower they were attending, just so I could experience that uniquely feminine event! And whenever I felt I could do it undetected, I dressed in the panties I hid under the mattress of my wife's and my bed, just to have some tangible connection to this confusing but insistent aspect of me. Since I was still years away from reading Dr. Paula Reeves' *Heart Sense*, I had no idea that these attractions to all things feminine were my heart's way of telling me about the much bigger truth of my essence as a person. Instead of recognizing my desires as my truth, I continued to see them as a weakness, a flaw, and I continued to beat myself up. "You're a phony, a fraud. People think you're a success, but you're nothing but a failure."

Eventually my inner turmoil began affecting my outer life. I was trying so hard to ignore what was going on inside me that it began to feel like I was living my life only for others, with no regard for my own needs. As a result, my emotional, physical, and spiritual well-being suffered. This created challenges in my marriage and family relationships. Repressing my gender dilemma caused me such pain that, true to the saying "Hurt people hurt others," I did things I am not proud of that hurt my wife and children. (Read more about this in chapter 4.) Internally, I struggled with anger and resentment. Even when I had not spoken hostile words, seeing my scowling face and furrowed brow would prompt my wife—and even others—to ask, "What's wrong? What are you mad about?" But I never knew how to answer them. And despite numerous career advancements and successes, there was always this feeling of lack and no sense of abundance.

Looking back, I now realize this turmoil was my heart's way of speaking to me through its second means of communication: the language of feelings. All these unpleasant feelings of anger, angst, and resentment contrasted sharply with the deep feelings of peace and contentment I had when I secretly dressed in feminine articles of clothing. Yet, still oblivious to the ways of the heart, I continued to ignore its wise counsel, all the time wondering why I had been cursed with this inexplicable burden. I prayed over and over for God to take these attractions from me. And when God did not, I wondered if, like the Apostle Paul, this was to be my unnamed "thorn in the flesh." I had no idea that these feelings I was having were my heart's attempt to speak to me about the truth of who God had created me to be.

Years passed. Personal computers became household items. The internet began connecting the world. And finally, when I was forty-five years old, I saw a website showing pictures of trans-gender women. In that moment, my heart spoke loud and clear through its third language—my intuition. I immediately recognized, "That's me!"

I spent the next five years doing online research, but the number of resources available then pales in comparison to what can be found now. Nevertheless, what little I did find kept me seesawing between the exhilaration of knowing "That's me!" and the despair of thinking, "I could never live my life as a WOMAN! What would God think? What would my family think? This whole idea is ridiculous!"

After five years on this emotional roller coaster, I came to two realizations. First, I recognized that, not only was I not happy, but with all my anger, angst, and hurtful actions, I was not contributing greatly to my loved ones' happiness either. Second, I realized that nothing was going to change until I made a decision. I had to decide whether to explore what my heart was saying or be forever stuck on the merry-go-round of "What ifs?"

Exploring My Feminine Side

In my online research, I began noticing more and more websites for dressing services—most of which were located in London, interestingly enough. One day I decided to Google "dressing service—Atlanta," and, to my surprise, a site popped up! The Explore Your Feminine Side website explained the services offered by a lovely, local woman named Ramona. I was enraptured by Ramona's description of how she would dress her clients in gorgeous women's clothes and complete our look with a feminine hairstyle and appropriate makeup. Once she transformed us into our beautiful selves, Ramona promised to coach us in feminine mannerisms.

She also said she would go to dinner with us so we could experience what it was like to be out in the world as a woman.

My heart was captivated by these words that so knowingly articulated my deepest longings and—for the first time—made these heart's desires feel surprisingly acceptable and actually attainable. Ramona offered support for what my heart had always longed to do, even when my head had not known where to begin. Presented with this opportunity, I chose to take a course of action I had feared for decades; I finally made the decision to explore my feminine side.

My hands shook as I dialed the number to make an appointment with Ramona. During that initial conversation, she asked me numerous questions. Had I chosen a name for myself? Did I know my bra size? My woman's shoe size? Despite the affirmation and authentication I experienced from Ramona's questions, when the day of the appointment finally arrived, I was just a hot mess driving to her home. But my butterflies quieted the moment Ramona opened the door and said, "Hi, Gabrielle." This was the first time anyone had ever called me by the feminine name I had chosen for myself. (See this book's introduction for that story.) Hearing "Gabrielle" brought me a deep sense of connection with the core of my being and a feeling of joyful anticipation. Ramona invited me to have a seat in her living room, where we proceeded to talk for a while. Even though I had arrived on her doorstep presenting in my handsome male persona, she explained that our time together that afternoon was going to be strictly girl time, totally Gabrielle time. That thought thrilled me to no end!

After we chatted some more, Ramona finally asked, "Are

you ready?"

"Yes!" I exclaimed. "I thought you'd never ask!"

Then Ramona ushered me upstairs to her dressing salon—and I thought I had died and gone to heaven! Her salon was several rooms full of dresses, shoes, wigs, jewelry, and drawers and drawers of lingerie! And that's where we started. The first thing Ramona pulled from those drawers was a pair of padded panties. She held them up, saying, "Gabrielle. Here's your butt."

"My butt?!?" I questioned. "I've already got a butt!"

"No," she said. "You don't have the right kind of butt. We're trying to create a feminine silhouette for you."

"Give me that butt," I said, grabbing it and pulling it on.

Ramona continued rummaging in her lingerie drawers. Coming up with two large silicone falsies, she announced, "Here's your boobs!" With that, I finally got the breasts I had always wanted—ever since I had first coveted my babysitter's bust line!

After Ramona got me all padded and dressed, she sat me down in her salon chair. Standing between me and the mirror, she did my makeup and added a wig—steps in the dressing process I had never done for myself. With her blocking my view, I couldn't see the metamorphosis taking place, and the butterflies from my drive over began fluttering anxiously. When Ramona finally finished, she again asked, "Are you ready?"

With my heart beating wildly, I replied, "I think so."

Then Ramona stepped away from the mirror, and there, for the very first time, I saw myself on the outside as the person I knew I was on the inside. I was 49 years old . . . and meeting myself for the very first time. My internal and external selves finally aligned, and deep down I knew; that *is* me.

This was such an emotional epiphany that I began to tear up, causing Ramona to exclaim, "Oh no, Gabrielle! Girl 101! If you're going to cry, you have to cry before I put the makeup on you . . . not after!"

．　　．　　．

For the next several months I would go to Ramona's every few weeks and have her work her transformational magic. During one of those sessions, Ramona told me about the Southern Comfort Conference—an international gathering of transgender individuals that took place in Atlanta every year. She said it was a space where I could live in my feminine essence for five days straight. That was all I needed to hear!

The Southern Comfort Conference (SCC) was another turning point in my journey. To be able to live in my truth for 120 uninterrupted hours gave me the opportunity to settle into my essence in a way that my three- to four-hour appointments with Ramona had not. SCC was also my first experience of seeing several hundred trans people all gathered in one place. This did so much to dispel my lifelong feelings of shame. Everywhere I turned I saw evidence that I was not alone; I was not the only person whose internal sense of my gender did not match my external anatomy.

Finding my tribe, my community, not only helped alleviate the shame I had felt in the past—it also gave me hope for the future. The beautiful women I met there—those who had been on this journey for a while and were living authentically in their feminine essence—showed me that it actually was possible to live life successfully as a transgender woman. But how could *I* ever do this? Meeting these trans women was like stepping onto an even bigger emotional roller coaster—one with steeper inclines and much scarier drops!

As the last day of the conference approached, I could not bear the thought of having to abandon my true essence and return to living in my old male persona. I felt like it would just kill me to have to stuff all these newly freed feelings of authenticity and internal-external alignment back into the tiny box of occasional appointments with Ramona. While my body would keep showing up—at home, at work, at church—I just knew my spirit would no longer be there.

When I shared my turmoil with Ramona, she said, "Gabrielle, if you really want to find out what moving forward as a woman might look like, I will help you. You can stay with me for a while and have access to all the clothes, shoes, wigs, makeup, jewelry— everything in my salon." I was overwhelmed—both by the gener- osity of her offer and by finding myself at the crossroads where it placed me. At that tender, fragile place, in the very beginning of my journey, I had the SCC-inspired hope of all I might gain by moving forward as a woman—coupled with the paralyzing fear of all I could lose. At the very top of that list was my family—the ones whom I loved with all my heart.

There are some trans individuals who come out to their families when they first begin exploring what it would mean to live as their authentic selves. But at that point in my life, I had absolutely no idea how to explain to my wife and children that I wanted—and actually needed—to live as a woman. I had no idea how to explain it to them because, quite frankly, I still didn't have the words to explain it to myself!

Remember what we learned from author Paula Reeves? Our heads speak in words and thoughts, but our hearts speak through feelings and intuitions. From the feelings of joy and alignment I had when dressing and interacting as a woman, I knew the truth of my being—that I am transgender. But because that knowing was coming from my heart, my head still needed time to learn how to articulate all this through its languages of thoughts and explanations. In other words, our hearts can know our truths long before our heads can explain them.

If you were sitting across from me right now, I would ask, "Can you relate to what I'm saying? Have you ever experienced a time when you knew you had to act on what your heart was telling you, but you were at a loss to explain the reasons for your actions?" Stop and think a moment. Do you know this feeling?

That was exactly where I found myself after talking to Ramona on the last day of the Southern Comfort Conference. Unfortunately, I was standing at this terrifying crossroads without the benefit of Paula Reeves's wisdom! Back then I knew so little about the workings of my heart that moving in any direction just felt scary and overwhelming. But even though I didn't know then how my heart communicated, it kept on speaking, compelling me forward.

My heart let me know, intuitively, that I still had no experiential knowledge of what living as Gabrielle would actually look like—or if I could even do that! Up to this point, all I knew about living as a woman was based on a few sessions with Ramona and five days at a conference surrounded by other trans people. Even at this early stage I could see that these experiences were a far cry from what it would be like living as a trans woman "in the real world." As my head sought explanations for the path my heart was considering, it began by posing logical questions: "Might this just be a phase? How can you be sure this is really you?" (Have you ever heard your head asking similar questions?) Having no solid answers made me realize I was not yet ready to try and explain this to my family. In order to find answers—for all of us—my heart knew I would have to spend time living, moving, and being in this world as a woman.

I also intuited that, in order to fully explore what living as a woman might look like, I would need a safe, supportive space where I could do this—exactly the sort of space Ramona was offering. And I knew my home could never be that place. Because my wife and I both adhered to the same conservative Christian beliefs I had been raised with, I was certain there was no way she would allow me to present as a woman in the privacy of our home, much less go out in public dressed as a woman.

Time has allowed my head to catch up with my heart so I can now articulate what I was intuiting. But I didn't have all these words back then. At that point, all I knew was that I was between a rock and a hard place. Accepting Ramona's offer meant risking everything—family, friends, career, church, relationship with God, reputation. But having tasted my truth, I knew there was no way I could ever function effectively—much less be happy and contribute to the well-being of others—by going back to my old male existence. For the many years before I knew what was going on inside me I had done my best to make my masculine incarnation work. But now that I had heard my heart's feminine truth, I knew that returning to my male persona would mean living a lie and existing outside my integrity. To go back to that, with this new awareness, felt like sentencing myself to life in prison; it felt like death.

With all these things jumbling in my mind—and with my hands shaking—the last thing I did before leaving my hotel room at the conference was make a heart-wrenching phone call to my wife. I told her I would not be home for a while. "I'm okay," I said. "I just need some time to find myself."

By then, September of 2010, all three of our children had graduated high school and were at various points in their college careers: just graduated, in school, and taking a gap year. Since my work often took me out of town for long stretches, my wife told the kids I was out of town working, and I began my life as Gabrielle. (See chapters 2, 4, and 5 for more about my family.) Because I was still employed, still supporting the family, and still not sure if I could actually live as a woman, I did continue working in my male persona. I would also present in male mode when I showed up at rare family events, like the fiftieth birthday party my wife threw for me, her father's funeral, and a hospital emergency room visit when one of my daughters was rushed there. But the rest of the time—most evenings, and definitely every weekend—I would dress and live as Gabrielle.

Living As Gabrielle

Along with opening her home and offering the resources of her salon, Ramona continued mentoring me in the fine art of feminine mannerisms. She taught me how to sit with my legs crossed and my knees together. She instructed me to take small bites instead of filling my mouth to capacity like a guy. Ramona taught me to walk gracefully—in heels, even!—and much, much more. She also noted that I was a very quick study and started reminding me to "man up" when I was in my male persona. Feminine mannerisms came so naturally to me that, even within my first year of being out, I would inevitably slip into them, regardless of whether I was presenting male or female.

As weeks went by, dressing in my male persona became increasingly burdensome—while expressing myself as Gabrielle brought me greater and greater joy. But my joy was severely impacted Memorial Day weekend of 2011, when Ramona was diagnosed with an aggressive brain tumor. Three months later, that tumor took her life.

Ramona's death was devastating to me. It is hard to put into words the depth of grief I felt over losing the person who had been both my midwife and mentor, helping me birth my true self, and then supporting me as I grew. I felt orphaned, bereft; for several weeks I could barely get out of bed. Then, as if that sorrowful burden was not enough to bear, several months later I lost my job. This ended up being one of the lowest points in my life. I was unemployed, still grieving Ramona's death, and would have been homeless, except for the kindness of a dear friend who let me crash on his sofa. I was still not out to my family and had no connection with any friends from my past. On top of all this, I had absolutely no idea how to make a living as a trans woman.

It is times like this when many transgender people attempt suicide. Statistics show that a staggering 40 percent of us try to take our own lives. That is dangerously close to half of us and a number that far exceeds the average American attempted suicide rate of 4.6 percent.[1] It is also a statistic that bleakly illustrates the overwhelming societal challenges faced by transgender people.

By the grace of God (more about that in chapters 2 and 3), when faced with all this loss, I did not become one of those statistics; but I knew I was in crisis. The Chinese symbol for crisis incorporates the signs for both danger and opportunity. I was very aware that all I had lost had put me in a very dangerous place. At the same time, I also realized it opened up an opportunity that I had only dreamed about . . . the opportunity to embrace my truth, once and for all, and live full-time as Gabrielle.

Since I had been working in my male persona for the two years I had been out, living full-time as Gabrielle would mean finding some way to earn an income as a 6'3" trans woman. But the thought of doing this was very scary! To understand my fear, you need to realize that the time period when I was wrestling with all this—the beginning of 2012—was

- *before* Caitlyn Jenner transitioned and appeared on the cover of *Vanity Fair,*

- *before* there were transgender characters on TV shows like *Glee, Orange Is the New Black, TransParent,* and *Pose,* and

- *before* transgender issues were appearing daily in our news feeds.

In the spring of 2012, many Americans knew next to nothing about transgender people. Consequently, I feared people would perceive me as a freak and not want to hire me. Also, the *Injustice at Every Turn* report released in 2011 showed that the study's almost 6,500 trans respondents experienced double the unemployment rate of the general population. Ninety percent of those who did have a job reported being harassed or mistreated in the workplace. Transgender people were also four times more likely than the general population to have a household income of less than $10,000 a year.[2]

Coupled with these daunting statistics was my firsthand knowledge, gained from over thirty years in the construction industry, that my good ol' boy colleagues would not welcome a trans woman showing up in their workplace—especially one who was arriving as their boss! On the other hand, I was disheartened by the thought of trading my six-figure income for a job flipping burgers or working at the local Walmart—if any of those places would even hire me!

Although the thought of trying to find work as a trans woman in 2012 was very scary (as it continues to be, for many gender diverse people today), the pastor of a trans welcoming church I had found wisely counseled me, "Gabrielle, you've got to keep moving forward." Then he shared a strategy with me. "List the things you know you can do and investigate those options." Well, I knew how to start a business. I also knew how to do home renovations and repairs, house cleaning, and lawn care and landscaping. So, as Gabrielle, I started a company for each. Slowly, through the support of new friends—many of whom were congregants of that trans welcoming church and others who were part of the LGBTQ community—and through lots and lots of hard work, my three businesses grew. I was able to support myself, although at a standard of living drastically lower than that which my six-figure income had afforded me.

Listening to my heart's invitation to live my truth full-time brought me greater happiness than I had ever known. On my way to church one Sunday morning, as I was driving away from my bleak, low-income, Section-8 apartment, I was overwhelmed by the irony of it all. For decades I had struggled and sacrificed, chasing the American dream. Our culture values affluence, achievement, and appearances—and I had gained all those things. But it was just as Jesus had warned his followers some 2,000 years earlier: I had gained the whole world, but lost my own soul (Matthew 16:26). Now, finally, I was listening to my heart and experiencing the true happiness I had always desired.

Throughout my life, my heart had beckoned me towards my truth—my happiness—through my ongoing attraction to feminine things. It had spoken to me through the feelings of peace I had when I secretly dressed in women's clothes, the longings I had to do the "girly" things my wife and daughters did, and the feelings of anger, angst, and resentment I experienced during the years of trying to repress my feminine essence. My heart guided me through my intuition when I was first coming out and led me to create a safe space where I could explore this fledgling side of myself.

Even as early as the age of six or seven, my heart had also been speaking to me through another one of its languages, a dream. In this nightmare my body inflated to a scary size and people shunned me because of the way I looked. I remember that dream vividly because I had it so frequently. It frightened me so much that my mom actually took me to see a doctor about it. Unfortunately, the doctor did not understand that this dream was my heart's way of speaking to me and helping me understand the challenges I would face in embracing my truth. He simply diagnosed me as having "too much stress" and sent me home.

Finally, during my adult years, my heart had also been speaking to me through its fifth language: my physical symptoms. For years I had experienced terrible cramping in my stomach. At least once a week the pain from the cramps would be so severe that I would end up vomiting; occasionally I actually passed out. After seeing several doctors I received a diagnosis of "spastic colon," but none of those medical professionals were ever able to recommend anything to relieve my intense cramps. Interestingly enough, within six months of deciding to live my truth full-time, my cramps went away, totally on their own, with no medication needed. After learning from Paula Reeves' *Heart Sense* book that physical symptoms are one of the heart's languages, a female friend commented, "Isn't it funny that your heart would use the singularly feminine symptom of cramps to show you your truth—that you are a woman!"

Of course, as you have seen in this chapter, it wasn't enough to just listen to my heart. I also had to act on what it was saying. That is where many of us get stuck—and where I stayed stuck for many years. Making changes in our lives can be very scary, so naturally we want some assurance that the risks will be worth it—a map with each turn in the road clearly marked. But that's not the way it worked for me. I had to take the first scary step before the second step appeared. I had to move forward on my journey, even though my destination was unknown. And in those times when I had no idea what the next step even looked like, I found that being willing to take a step, being willing to make a change, opened up opportunities that had not previously presented themselves.

If your heart is speaking to you about an aspect of your life that is waiting to unfold, you may feel stuck and afraid, just like I did. If so, I encourage you to be willing to make a change, and then to watch for little things you can do to move in that direction. You don't have to wait until your head can explain everything before you act on what your heart knows. If we just keep taking even the tiniest of steps, we will soon find ourselves making progress on the journey of embracing our truths.

Your Turn
EMBRACE YOUR TRUTH EXERCISE #1
Discover What Your Heart Is Saying

Because this is both a book about my journey and an invitation for you to embrace your truth more fully, at the end of each chapter, I will invite you to engage in some sort of exercise or activity. The following activity is designed to help you listen to your heart and uncover some of the unlived facets of your truth. I use the phrase "unlived facets" because I believe that the truth of each of our lives is multifaceted and that there are always more aspects of our truth waiting to be discovered and lived—for our own well-being and for the healing of our world.

To begin discovering more of the brilliant facets of your life, I invite you to complete these sentences. If you are not ready to do this exercise right now, I encourage you to not read it now, but simply skip it, for the moment, and come back to it when you have fifteen or twenty minutes to devote to it.

NOTE: Please do NOT read through this exercise before doing it. It is most effective when you simply answer the questions, one at a time, in order.

1. Someone I admire is _____

_____

2. What I MOST admire about that person is _____

_____

3. Another person I admire is _____

_____

4. What I MOST admire about that person is _____

_____

Now think about some unexplored attraction in your life . . . some place you have yet to visit, something you have yet to check into, some activity you have been interested in but have yet to try. Now write:

5. Something I'm attracted to is _____

_____

6. Some other thing I'm attracted to is_____

_____

7. A third thing I'm attracted to is _____

_____

8. A physical symptom I've been having is _____

_____

9. The theme of a recurring dream I've had is (Write just a one-line summary of the theme of these dreams, not all the details.) _____

_____

_____

_____

Our dreams, attractions, feelings, intuitions, and physical symptoms are like the warning lights on our dashboards, signaling us to pay attention to important messages from our heart. With that in mind . . .

- Consider the possibility that the things you admire most in people are actually your heart's way of letting you know that this quality or ability is a part of you, a facet of your brilliant self that is waiting to be brought forth and embraced.

- Consider that the things you're attracted to are also a part of your unique truth, that they are things that could bring greater fulfillment to you and greater joy to the world.

- What might the theme of your recurring dream be telling you about your truth?

- What might your heart be trying to say through your physical symptoms?

Returning to your answers to questions 1–9, consider them from the perspective that they are messages from your heart about the truth of your being. Write down any insights that come to you. _____

_____

_____

_____

_____

To learn more about how to listen to your heart, I encourage you to read *Heart Sense: Unlocking Your Highest Purpose and Deepest Desire,* by Paula Reeves, PhD.

TWO

Build a Support System

Embracing our truth inevitably involves making changes in our lives. In some cases, it may require making only minor adjustments in our daily routines—get up thirty minutes earlier to meditate, get in a quick workout, or fix a healthy breakfast. In my case, it led to major changes in every aspect of my life. The magnitude of the changes needed will depend on the size of the truth we are laboring to bring forth. Likewise, the size of the network needed to support us in our metamorphosis increases in proportion to the magnitude of the changes that must be made. Needless to say, doing all that was required to birth my true gender identity necessitated a very large support system. As I share my experiences of building that system, I invite you to consider where you might find support for birthing the next brilliant facet of your truth—the facet that may be just waiting to shine forth.

Ramona

In 2010, when I finally began focusing on embracing my truth, I was blessed with support on numerous fronts. Initially, Ramona was my main support person.

Ramona was a classy woman in her vintage years whose dating profile read "a Southern lady with an eclectic side." Part of her eclectic nature came from the company she kept; while Ramona identified as a straight, cisgender woman, she had many friends in the LGBTQ community. Several years before we met, Ramona had been at a bar one evening, chatting with a friend. This friend shared that they were a cross-dresser who struggled with getting their feminine presentation just right. Being a stylish, kind-hearted person with a college art degree, Ramona said, "I'd like to help you with that."

When she did, her friend was thrilled with the results, exclaiming, "You could make a living doing this!" Even though she was a successful realtor, the idea intrigued her. Seeing the positive impact her assistance had on her friend inspired Ramona to help more people. She purchased dresses, lingerie, jewelry, wigs, breast forms, makeup in different shades, and high heels in women's sizes 10–14. Then Ramona created her Explore Your Feminine Side website. The compelling way she described the experience one would have of connecting with their feminine side kept her phone ringing off the hook with calls from new clients. By the time I came across Ramona's site, her business had already been thriving for a year or two, serving mostly successful, married, well-to-do businessmen.

Along with giving me a place to live and instructing me

in feminine mannerisms, Ramona also taught me the fine art of putting on makeup. She was the one who told me how to create the illusion of lush, full lips, where to put the blush on my cheeks, why I needed bronzer, and which brush to use for what. And Ramona was endlessly patient. More than once I remember coming downstairs after spending forty minutes doing my makeup, only to have her take one look and gently suggest, "Why don't you go back upstairs and try again."

Ramona helped this college math major figure out the conversion formula between male and female sizes . . . both for clothes and for shoes. She also mentored me in other intricacies of dressing as a woman. Who knew that men and women thread their belts in opposite directions—and that our waistlines are located in different places? As a guy, I wore my pants at the top of my hips, but as a woman, I was to wear my skirts at my belly button!

I was blessed to know Ramona for seventeen months before she died. Along with being the best mentor a trans woman could have, she also helped me develop a social support system. Ramona introduced me to her clients—cross-dressers and transgender individuals who were taking steps to embrace their truths. These new friends taught me much about the joys of going out in public as my true self—which actually did require some learning on my part! The very first time I went out dressed as Gabrielle I was so terrified someone would recognize me that I barely remember any details of that momentous experience. But in the company of my new support system, I gradually learned to relax and enjoy being in public as my authentic self. For someone who had spent almost forty years stealing moments of dressing as her true self only in private, this was a huge step on the journey of embracing my truth.

The Atlanta TGs

The Atlanta TGs were another group that provided me with much support. They were a Meetup group, consisting mostly of trans women, who met monthly for a social excursion. With the TGs I experienced one of the rites of passage for every trans woman; my first outing in a bikini. For me, and for many of my trans sisters, being able to dress in bikinis and evening gowns are singularly feminine experiences that we have longed to indulge in since we were little girls—always mistakenly dressed as boys. Consequently, I was very excited, yet also anxious, about my first opportunity to wear a two-piece bathing suit. At that time, my bosom was an optical illusion created by breast forms. These were two silicone blobs, each shaped like a breast, that trans women and female breast cancer survivors position in their bras to create a bosom. My anxiety came from questions like, "Would my bikini top hold the weight of my breast forms? Would the forms slide around when swimming and end up sticking out of my top? Did my 6'3" body look feminine enough?" Worried by these misgivings, it was a relief to know that at least I would be having my first bikini experience with the support of the TGs. It was good to be in the company of those who understood my fears and who would be compassionate about any wardrobe malfunctions!

Fortunately, I had no bikini mishaps that day, and my TG sisters and I enjoyed a very pleasant houseboat outing. The houseboat actually belonged to a dear friend of mine who had generously offered to allow our group to spend the day on his boat. The

TGs had such a good time that day and were so impressed with my ability to arrange for this excursion that they appointed me as their official event coordinator. As a person who was used to using leadership skills in her male persona, it was very affirming to me, as a woman, to be invited to use these skills in service to my sisters. As Gabrielle, I welcomed this opportunity to be able to give something back to my new community.

City of Light Atlanta

While I was grateful for the TGs, for Ramona, and for the friends I had made through her, I was missing my church and my relationship with God. Up until I began transitioning, God and the church had always been an integral part of my support system. But when I began my transition, I did not know how to be trans, a Christian, and a church-goer—all at the same time. So along with putting my relationship with my family on hold for a season, the only way I knew how to explore my feminine self was to put God and the church on hold as well.

In 2011—about a year after I had first come out and before Ramona had passed—one of my new friends, a cross-dresser named Rhonda, told me about First Metropolitan Community Church (now City of Light Atlanta). She said it was a local congregation that was trans welcoming. I so wanted to check out that church, but I first had to fight through my fear of what people would think about a 6'3" trans woman showing up for their worship service. I also had to work through my fear of what God would think! Finally, I mustered up the courage to attend the Easter morning service there. I can gladly say, that decision changed my life.

Although I didn't hear anything new during worship, I felt new things. I finally felt the joy of connecting with my Creator as my true self, internally and externally aligned. This was the most profound spiritual experience I had ever had. That morning, I also felt the warm welcome of a spiritual community. At the end of the service, as Ramona and I were trying to duck out unnoticed, the senior pastor, Rev. Dr. Paul Graetz, caught us at the door. Looking me right in the eye, he said how nice it was to see me and actually encouraged me to come back. I had to pinch myself to make sure I wasn't dreaming!

It turned out that Pastor Paul had really meant what he said, and that his parishioners were as warmly welcoming as their pastor. Over the next few years, I was invited to bring my gifts of ministry to that congregation. I joined the choir, which I ended up directing for a season, and started a transgender support group at the church. The women's softball coach invited me and several other trans congregants to join the team. I was even elected to serve on the church's executive board. There I was able to put my thirty years in the construction industry to good use as chair of the Building and Grounds Committee.

That congregation supported me in other ways as well. Their welcoming of my new self and their valuing of all my old abilities—my singing voice, leadership skills, athletic talent, and knowledge of construction—helped me explore how my past and present fit together. This enabled me to feel like one whole person instead of two separate people.

Pastor Paul's partner, Robert, also became a key person in my support system. Among his many talents, Robert is a gifted hair stylist. He mentored me though the awkward stages of growing my hair out from its short, masculine cut to a more feminine, below-the-shoulders length. Robert instructed me in the art of styling my hair and, with his coloring magic, gradually transitioned me from a graying, dark-haired man to a beautiful blonde woman. If I had a special occasion to attend, I would go to Paul and Robert's house. There, Robert would always create a stunning look for me, just for that evening. Knowing the financial challenges I was experiencing, he generously offered me his services for free or, at the most, for a miniscule fraction of what I would have paid at a salon. Robert was a tremendous help to me in the early years of my transition, and I was truly blessed to have him as part of my support system.

When Ramona was diagnosed with her brain tumor, the City of Light congregation rallied around us with constant support. Paul and Robert often drove Ramona to her chemo treatments while I was at work. When she died, Ramona's estranged family would not permit any cross-dressers or trans individuals at her funeral. Knowing how deeply we were grieving, Pastor Paul held a second memorial service at City of Light. This gave our community the much-needed opportunity to come together to celebrate the life of this incredibly gracious, gifted "eclectic Southern lady" who had done so much for so many of us.

Out of the many acts of comfort and encouragement I experienced from this congregation, one in particular stands out in my mind. The first Sunday I came back to worship after Ramona passed, it was all I could do to drag my grieving self out of bed and get my body to church. Feeling fragile and emotionally unsteady, I slipped in and took a seat on the back row. Within minutes, I had dissolved into tears. One of the congregants, someone I barely even knew then, slid over, put their arm around me, and just let me cry. Leslie never said a thing, but their embodied act of kindness spoke healing to my heart more effectively than any words ever could.

After Ramona's death and the loss of my job, as I was trying to figure out how to live my truth full-time and make a living as a trans woman, Pastor Paul was the minister who encouraged me to write a list of everything I knew how to do. He counseled me to keep moving, doing one of those things from the list. Upon starting my cleaning company, lawn care service, and home renovation business, the members of City of Light became some of my very first clients. Another church friend generously provided financial support that helped move my companies from fledgling to flourishing.

Pastor Paul, Robert, and other members of the congregation soon became not just my friends, but my "family"—the people I spent time with on a regular basis. With all the activities I was involved in, and because I lived in close proximity to the church, I was there almost every day. This meant I would often grab a meal with these friends before or after worship, board meetings, softball games, choir rehearsals, classes, or trans support group meetings, or in the midst of working on a building and grounds project.

It's hard to put into words how vital and life affirming it was to find a supportive spiritual community so early in my journey. Starting from the time when I was still living a double life, going back and forth between working in my male persona and living as Gabrielle, this congregation gave me some much-needed space to develop my experiential knowledge of being a woman. The experiences I had at City of Light—working, learning, playing, and worshipping together—made it possible for me to know what it truly felt like—how it actually resonated, in the depths of my being—to fully live as a woman. At last, my essence was having the opportunity to align with my experiences. Having this experiential knowledge gave my head the words it needed to explain the truth of my heart. And being invited to contribute out of my essence, to serve the congregation in various capacities, assured me of what I most needed to know: that I could not only live as a woman, but I could actually make a difference as a woman. For me, this was the frosting on the cake, the icing without which the cake could have been enjoyed, but it wouldn't have tasted nearly as sweet.

To help you understand another dimension of what being accepted by this congregation meant to me, imagine what your life would be like if you felt you could only live the truth of your being in secret, if you feared you would be shunned and ostracized by anyone who knew your truth. Imagine the shame—the feelings of being intrinsically unacceptable, unworthy, and unlovable—that would worm their way into your soul if you spent forty years fearing you would be rejected and ridiculed by others if you ever showed your real face in public. Then, imagine bringing your frightened, fearful, but authentic self to not just one person, not just two people, but to a whole community. Imagine all those people welcoming you with open hearts and embracing you with open arms. Imagine those community members caring about your well-being, hearing your story with open minds, and trusting you enough to elect you to a position of leadership. Imagine what that would do to you; imagine what that would do for you.

That is what City of Light did for me. This welcoming and accepting spiritual community was not only life giving to me; it was also life saving. When I was at my lowest point, after Ramona's death—when I had also lost my job and had no place to live—the tremendous support I received from this spiritual community was the main reason I did not attempt suicide. I only wish that the 40 percent of my trans siblings who have tried to take their lives could have experienced similar support from a loving community. Statistics show that the support of a loving family can literally mean the difference between life and death for a young trans person.[3] The loving church family I found at City of Light certainly made that difference for me.

Linda

In September of 2012, a new person joined the City of Light staff, someone who was destined to become another integral member of my support system. Rev. Linda Herzer is a straight, White, middle-class, cisgender woman who has a real heart for the LGBTQ community. When she joined the staff, Linda knew very little about transgender people but was eager to learn. Soon after she started working at the church, Linda invited me over to her place saying, "I'll fix dinner if you'll tell me your story."

That ended up being the first of many deep, rich conversations. In an attempt to support me in my journey, Linda began sharing wisdom and experiences from her own life. It turned out that we had much in common. There was just a one year difference in our ages, we both had kids in their twenties, and we were both just two years into some major life changes. In 2010, the same year I first came out, Linda had left a ten-year career as a school librarian to return to her first love: working with adults around issues of personal and spiritual growth. Her vocational journey had gone by fits and starts since then, as had mine. She had just separated from her husband of twenty-plus years, so we were both struggling to navigate new terrain with our spouses and children. Since childhood, we had both had a deep, meaningful relationship with God. Church had always been an integral part of our lives, and she knew as many old gospel songs as I did. Because of our life circumstances, City of Light became "family" for both of us, and each of us was there whenever the doors were open. Since we lived near each other and money was tight for both of us, we would often carpool to church events to save on gas.

When we weren't at the church, Linda and I spent time sharing dinners and deep conversation on the little balcony of her apartment. We would talk for hours, enjoying views of the Midtown Atlanta skyline through the trees. Linda's accepting spirit, attentive listening, and knack for asking insightful questions prompted me to share on a deeper level than I had ever revealed myself before. When I would marvel at the depth of our sharing and the connection developing between us, Linda would laugh and say, "Girl, this is just what women DO!"

And so it was, for her—a cisgender woman who had grown up having close female friends. But for me—a transgender woman who had spent most of my life experiencing friendships as a guy— this was all new. Living in male mode, my friendships with other guys had revolved mainly around activities in which we were participating. Those friendships did not involve sharing feelings and being vulnerable with one another. While my wife had been my best friend, I had also approached that friendship from a guy's social conditioning. Consequently, I would share some of what was going on with me, but generally, I tried to be strong for her. I would listen to her struggles, but, like many men, I tried not to burden her with my worries and concerns.

Of course, Ramona had become a good friend in the seventeen months I knew her. But since her expertise had been in helping me develop my external feminine expression, the focus of our friendship had been on outward things. Linda was the one who opened the way for me to explore my internal feminine essence.

Initially Linda did this by just being herself, a highly introspective, deeply centered woman who knows and values her own feminine essence. The more time I spent around her, at the church and one on one, the more I experienced the feminine way in which she nurtures others. I saw her listen deeply and graciously hold space for people's growth. I watched her do quiet little acts of kindness to provide people the support they needed, just when they needed it. I'll never forget the time Linda, several other parishioners, and I rushed Pastor Paul to the emergency room. Paul was experiencing excruciating abdominal pain that was later diagnosed as kidney stones. Once he got into a room, Paul asked the nurse if she had a heating pad he could use to mitigate the pain. She said, "No," and left to attend to other patients. Without saying a word, Linda went to work. She turned off the overhead lights so they wouldn't be glaring in Paul's eyes. She poked around in the room's supply closet where she found a blanket. Linda instructed me to put this over Paul to keep him warm. Continuing her search, she found a rubber surgical glove. Filling that with hot water, Linda tied it off like a balloon and presented Paul with a makeshift hot water bottle in lieu of a heating pad. These were the feminine acts of nurturing kindness that flowed from her constantly. These were the things that called forth my desire to get more in touch with my own feminine essence.

When I shared this desire with Linda, she—being an avid reader and former librarian—went looking for a good book to help me connect with my femininity. The book Linda found was better than good; for me, it was life changing! Not only did that book's author impact me profoundly, but she became the first of many insightful writers whom I would add to my support system.

Authors

In 1993, Marianne Williamson published *A Woman's Worth.* She had written it to encourage predominantly straight, certainly cisgender women to recognize and honor both their own feminine essence and the strengths of all women. I am sure when Marianne published this book she had no idea how helpful it would be, twenty years later, to a transgender woman seeking to connect more deeply to her feminine essence!

From Marianne Williamson I first learned the importance of feelings and how honoring them contributes to our well-being. I learned how strong one has to be to just listen to another's problems—and not try to fix them. Marianne taught me the importance of holding space for people, as a pregnant woman holds space for her unborn child. An expectant mother nurtures her baby, but mostly provides room in her womb for them to grow in their own way, according to their own wisdom and design.

Like a tuning fork inviting musicians to find their own pure note, Marianne's words helped connect me, on a deeper level, to my pure feminine essence. Having the words to now articulate these various aspects of my essence made me more confident in my femininity. They allowed me to embrace it more fully and settle into it more deeply. Likewise, the clearer my note became, the more I noticed that, when it comes to embracing our truth, we are all musicians. As each of us finds our own pure note, together we create the brilliant harmonies and counterpoints that transform the chaotic noise in our world into a beautiful symphony.

I was so excited about Marianne's book that I wanted a chance to discuss it with other women. I convinced Linda to co-lead a women's book group with me at the church. Through that discussion group, I ended up adding other life-changing authors and their books to my support network: Louise Hay's *You Can Heal Your Life*, Paula Reeves's *Heart Sense* (referenced in chapter 1), Edwene Gaines's *The Four Spiritual Laws of Prosperity*, and Don Miguel Ruiz's *The Four Agreements*, to name just a few. Several years later, through my participation in another book group, Brené Brown and Tama Kieves joined the ranks of authors whose wisdom continues to have a profound influence on my life.

Elizabeth

Along with introducing me to authors who became a significant part of my support system, Linda also connected me to my first life coach, Elizabeth Malone. How Elizabeth and I met is a funny story. One of the women from our church, Andrea, decided to host a women's retreat in the North Georgia mountains. Linda planned to attend, and, since we were good friends, she asked me to go too.

One of the things I love about Linda is that she has always seen me as "just one of the girls." Consequently, she invited me to this "Harnessing Your Divine Feminine" retreat in the same spirit that she invited some of her other girlfriends to attend, thinking nothing of it. Little did she know that her invitation left me "quaking in my boots" (or, more aptly, my stilettos)! The thought of spending a whole weekend surrounded by cisgender women thrilled and terrified me . . . in equal measures! Would I fit in and feel like "one of the girls," or would I feel like an outsider—or worse yet, an imposter? Would these women accept me as one of them, or view me as an interloper? Despite my fears, I signed up for the retreat. I didn't share my reservations with Linda until we were driving to the mountains that weekend. Her genuine surprise that I would even have such feelings quieted my fears.

We arrived safely, got settled into our rooms, met the other women, and shared a wonderful meal. Encouraged by the warm and welcoming energy of the ladies I met, I was starting to think that all would be well. Then Andrea introduced that speaker for the evening: Elizabeth Malone, a life coach who specialized in helping women reclaim their feminine moxie. Her topic for the evening: "How to Get Your Sexy Back!" When I heard the workshop's title I felt like I had just been thrown into the deep end, and I was about to discover if I could swim!

We had quite a time that night. There was lots of laughter and heartfelt sincerity as we shared aloud our definitions of sexy and what made us feel sexy. We danced our sexy and discussed our sexy, and contemplated it from perspectives from which I had never considered it before! For most of the women, it was a hilarious, heartfelt time of bonding. For me, it's harder to describe all that it was—a trial by fire, an initiation into the blessed mysteries of sisterhood, and more. Whatever it was, by the end of the evening, I knew I belonged; on a deeper level than ever before, I knew I was home.

After that evening, I felt there was more I could learn from Elizabeth, so I began seeing her for life coaching. While Marianne Williamson had begun my education on the importance of listening to my feelings, Elizabeth took this training to a whole new level. I will share more about this in chapter 6, but for now, suffice it to say that for the next twelve months, Elizabeth became a vital part of my support system.

Scott

My dear friend Scott is another invaluable member of my support network. I got to know Scott back in 2010, when I first came out. He was the tall, dark, handsome bartender—with a wicked sense of humor—at ROXX, one of the LGBTQ restaurants near Ramona's neighborhood. After she died, ROXX became my *Cheers*, the bar in the old TV sitcom, where I went because—true to that show's theme song—everybody knew my name . . . and they were always glad I came. While I was sitting there at the bar, Scott and I became friends. He would try out his newest drink creation on me and tell me his joke of the day, while I shared the ups and downs of my life with him. With all the kidding around he did, it was easy to see Scott as just some easy-going, fun-loving guy. But I soon came to know him as a wise soul with a heart of gold—the brother I never had.

During that lowest point in my life, when I was jobless and grieving Ramona's death, I got into a very unhealthy, unpleasant living situation. Things started going south soon after I moved in, and finally things came to a head. I knew I had to get out of there right then—but it was 3:00 in the morning! Having no place to go and no money to get me anywhere, I called Scott and told him my plight. Without hesitation he responded, "Pack your things. I'm coming to get you." Within three hours, I was out of that mess and safe in the refuge of Scott's apartment.

During the months I crashed on Scott's sofa, I was wrestling with making the decision to find work as a trans woman so I could live my truth 24/7. Throughout this tenuous time, Scott was always accepting of me; he was always there to support and encourage me. Scott also knew how to lighten the mood and keep me from taking myself too seriously. One day he came home from work and found my breast forms sitting on top of the dryer. Loving a good practical joke, Scott took a photo of my falsies and posted it on Facebook with the caption, "Where's Gabrielle?!?"

Scott also had the wisdom to know when it was time to nudge me out of his nest so I could learn to fly. After three months, he gently encouraged me to find my own place and helped me look for an apartment. When I finally moved out, he let me keep my tools and lawn equipment in his garage for several more years—

and never once charged me any rent or storage fees.

Since I had absolutely no household items when I moved into my apartment, a church friend loaned me some furniture, linens, and kitchen things she had in storage, and I set up housekeeping. It was low-income housing with noisy neighbors, paper-thin walls, and more bugs than I preferred, but it was all mine. During the four years I was there someone committed suicide in the apartment behind me, there were numerous police raids, and the kids in the complex burned down a storage shed. Yet, I am eternally grateful to Scott for helping me find that affordable apartment and for being my knight in shining armor when I needed rescuing. To this day, he is still one of my dearest friends and closest confidantes, and I am so blessed to have him as part of my support system.

Family

NOTE: Throughout this book I have used the names of friends but changed the names of all family members to protect their privacy.

I think it is fair to say that, on some level, all human beings long for the support of their families. But it is often difficult for loved ones to immediately get on board with their trans family member. As much as coming to terms with my gender identity has been a journey for me, it has also been a journey for those who had a relationship with me prior to transitioning. In the same way that I needed time to come to understand that I was trans, my family members need time to do their processing as well. I learned that if I was to hope for support from my family, then I must first hold space for them to do their grieving, to figure out what my transition means for them.

While this is the wisdom I developed over time, in the beginning of my transition, I was simply terrified that my family would reject me. You may recall that my dad was a Pentecostal preacher, so my mom was a pastor's wife. Both my wife and I had been leaders in our church, and we had raised our children in that conservative congregation. My fear of rejection, and the fact that I myself barely understood what living my life as a woman would be like, were the two things that kept me from telling my family what was going on with me in 2010, the year I began exploring my female gender identity in a public way.

Although I had not planned it like this, the first family member I came out to was my youngest daughter, Mandy. In the spring of 2012, Mandy was twenty-one years old and a contestant in an out-of-state competition. Since her mom was working and I was unemployed, I was the one who took her to the event—in male mode, of course. It had been nineteen months since I had stopped living at home, and Mandy—who had been living there during some of that time—was no longer buying the story that I was "out of town working." On the drive home, she began asking questions. "Dad, what's going on with you? I know something's going on. Tell me what it is." As my daughter continued to grill me, I finally broke down. Through my tears, I told her all that had been happening in my life. She was shocked, but gracious and supportive. Mandy said she wanted to know more, so we scheduled a time for her to meet and go out with Gabrielle. From this beginning, our relationship has continued to evolve and strengthen through both of our intentional efforts. Mandy herself captured and celebrated the strength of our bond in a note I received from her recently. She wrote,

> *You are a safe place for me. When I am around you I feel understood and unconditionally loved. You are full of so much wisdom and I know that I can call you whenever I am in need of honest and good advice. I am so grateful that our relationship has gotten stronger the past few years . . . I love you so much and I am so happy you are my parent.*

It is hard to express how much these words meant to me, how extremely grateful I am for Mandy's ongoing support, and how blessed I am by the close relationship we have today. It is also hard to put into words the tremendous relief I felt, eight years ago, having a family member be so accepting of me from the very beginning. I knew from other trans friends that immediate acceptance from loved ones is not to be expected; it is the exception, not the rule.

Several months after coming out to Mandy, I came out to my wife, Judy. During the almost two years since I made the call telling her that I needed to find myself, we had minimal contact. If there was a problem at the house—the yard needed attention or something needed to be repaired—Judy would call me and I would scrub off my nail polish, pull my lengthening hair back into a pony tail, throw on the few male clothes I still owned, and go take care of it.

The day I finally came out to Judy we met for lunch at a restaurant where Mandy was working. During the course of the meal, our daughter came to our table and asked, "Have you told her yet?"

"Told me what?" questioned my wife.

That's when I finally shared my truth with her. Judy was totally blindsided: shocked, angry, and understandably hurt. Through her tears, she told me this made our marriage feel like a lie. Her words immediately activated the voice of my ever-present Internal Accuser: "See! You really are a fraud, a failure! Look at what you've done to this woman whom you vowed to love and cherish 'til death do you part." In the midst of my own shame and feelings of failure, I tried to assure her that I had always truly loved her. I know she heard what I was saying, but I also know she certainly wasn't feeling it—not that day, and not for a long time to come. Over the eight years since then, we have been able to find our way back to an amicable relationship—never again as husband and wife, but as two people who still care deeply for each other and who continue to share the joys and challenges of parenting our adult children.

A few months after I came out to Judy, my older daughter learned about Gabrielle when she found my page on Facebook. (More about this in chapter 5.) I deeply regret that I had not been proactive and told her sooner, in person.

I also regret that I did not come out to my son until about a year after that. Because Jason and I had been very close, and I knew how much he looked up to me, I was terrified that learning my truth might do irreparable harm to our relationship. That is part of the reason it took me so long to come out to him. In fact, my guess is that it was probably his mom or one of his sisters who actually broke the news to him, but he never let on if they did. In December of 2013, I texted Jason and asked if he would be willing to see me, to meet me at my local Starbucks. He agreed. What I didn't know was that his sisters had decided to come with him, to offer support for both of us. It was wonderful to see the three of them arrive together that cool December day! This was the first time Jason had ever met Gabrielle in person, so I spent a lot of time explaining, in a choked-up voice, all that had been going on with me in the last three years, and even prior to that. Jason didn't interrupt or ask questions; he just silently took it all in. When I finally wound down, I recall that Mandy was the first to speak. As was often the case, she cracked a joke that got us all laughing and shifted the energy. We spent the rest of the time catching up on what was new with each of them and cutting up and having fun, just like old times. Well . . . almost like old times. A major change had taken place, and finally we all knew it.

I have reached out to my parents numerous times. However, they—and my sister—have chosen not to see me since someone told them about my transition eight years ago. My parents' lack of responsiveness—to texts, calls, a letter, and even to birthday cards and Mother's and Father's Day greetings—has been heartbreaking to me. I honestly cannot think of anything one of my children could do that would cause me to sever ties with them. Several years ago, as I was trying to come to terms with my parents' actions, I received very wise counsel from another spiritual mentor, Rev. Dr. David Ault. "Gabrielle, having you in their life would greatly challenge your parents' lifelong religious beliefs. It would require them to rethink the deep convictions that have undergirded their lives for decades. It is extremely hard for people to go there." Rev. David's words helped me find peace in my heart and empowered me to keep hoping that one day they will want to reconnect. I continue, to this day, to hold space for them.

In December of 2014, one of my cousins learned of my true gender identity at a family gathering. Soon thereafter, Tami reached out to me on Facebook, with the words, "I choose love." I have to confess, having experienced no support from my extended family up to this point, I was skeptical of her intentions. However, Tami assured me that she was indeed acting out of love, so we set up a time to meet for dinner. We spent hours catching up that evening. Much had transpired, in both our lives, since we had drifted apart as young adults with growing families.

That dinner date became the first of many gatherings with my kind, deep, open-minded, supportive, fun-loving cousin. Getting to add this life-giving woman of God to my support system has been a wonderful blessing. Her husband and sons have also embraced me, and Tami has reconnected me with several other family members as well. Through her, I now have some accepting, extended family who are actually blood relatives. The support of all these individuals has been grounding, affirming, and life enriching to me. I am so grateful to have each of them in my life.

Grateful

The major life changes I had to make in order to embrace the truth of my gender identity required a wide support system, which I have been blessed to find. I know I would not be the woman I am today, nor be doing all the things I am doing, if it were not for each and every one of these groups and individuals who provided me with the support that was so vital to me in the early years of my transition. As my journey has continued, I have been blessed to connect with more wonderful, supportive friends and I am deeply grateful for them, as well.

Your Turn
Embrace Your Truth Exercise #2
Develop a Support System

At the beginning of this chapter, I stated that, whenever we want to embrace some new facet of our truth, it is helpful to create a support system. Consequently, I encourage you to spend time thinking and perhaps writing about this. Where might you find support for the unlived facets of your truth, the truth your heart is now inviting you to bring forth?

If you are wanting to make a career change, are there local networking groups with which you could get involved? Could you find a running buddy, a friend to join you at the gym, or a nutritionist who could support you in taking better care of your body? Is there a class you could join to explore an awakening creative aspect, a Meetup group you could connect with to develop a new hobby or interest, or a spiritual community, counselor, and/or life coach who could help you with your personal growth? And don't forget to include authors and bloggers and YouTube gurus in your new support system!

I invite you to jot down some of your ideas here. Beside each idea, also write a date by which you intend to connect with this source. Remember, our intentions require our actions in order to become our reality!

Source of Support   Contact Date

_____

_____

THREE

Learn to Love Yourself

Embracing our truths does not always bring us accolades and approval from others. That is why, along with developing a support system, we must also learn to love ourselves. On those days when we receive little or no affirmation from the outside world, we have to be able to look within and like what we see. This is something I learned early on in the journey of embracing my authenticity— and a lesson that became a journey in and of itself.

Mirror Work

"I love you. Gabrielle, I love you."

This is what I would tell myself every morning as I rolled out of bed. Catching my reflection in the mirrored closet doors of my bleak little apartment, I would say, "Gabrielle, I love you."

This was the "alone" phase of my journey—after Ramona

died and I had moved out of Scott's place, but before I met Linda—when I was still in the process of developing my support system. It wasn't that I was lonely. I hung out with friends from church and my new friends in the trans community. I could usually find Scott behind the bar at ROXX and would go there to joke around with him and the rest of the gang. But I had yet to develop any of these friendships into deep, close relationships—the kind where you share your heart and soul on a regular basis. So there was no one I felt comfortable calling, in the middle of the night, when doubts arose. *Am I doing the right thing? Will I be able to make this month's rent? Will my family ever accept me? Am I going to be okay?* There was no one to help shield me from the constant barrage of scathing texts I received from those who knew me pretransition, telling me I was selfish, deceived by Satan, and worse. I felt alone, and I had to dig deep to find the self-love I needed to keep going.

What inspired me to dig deep was the love I experienced from the people at my new church. For me, those congregants were "God with skin on." Their acceptance enabled me to believe that God loved the real me, Gabrielle. This fragile belief was fuel for the journey of learning to love myself.

The mirrored closet doors in my new apartment provided the first opportunity for me to practice self-love. I have to confess, I was a bit obsessed with those full-length mirrored doors; I never tired of seeing my true self reflected there! I know this could sound vain and egotistical, but honestly, it was more like the magnetic attraction a parent has for their newborn's face. Like an adoring parent, awestruck by their infant, I was mesmerized by the image I saw in my mirror. And in the same way a parent whispers endearments to their baby, I started speaking softly to my reflection, "Gabrielle, I love you. Gabrielle, I love you." Doing that felt so good that I did it more and more, and with greater and greater intention. Eventually, looking myself in the eyes and telling myself, "Gabrielle, I love you," became a daily practice for me.

But after a particularly anxious night, or an early morning condemning text, I didn't always feel like engaging in my new daily practice. Those were the mornings I had to dig even deeper to connect with self-love. Knowing I wanted to shake off feelings of anxiety and condemnation and get back to a warm, loving state, I would go to the closet doors, look myself in the eyes, and begin my practice. "Gabrielle, I love you. Gabrielle, I love you." As I continued saying this, over and over, I would sink into this truth and feel the love. Somehow, I knew it was not enough just to *say* the words; I needed to *feel* them, too. It was both having the thought *and* experiencing the feeling that empowered me to resist frequent temptations to succumb to fear and anxiety, to guilt and shame. Synchronizing my thoughts and feelings enabled me to build a solid foundation of self-love.

Those mirrored closet doors were truly a gift to me—as was the picture window in the apartment downstairs. I would catch my reflection in that window, and tell myself, "You can do this! It's gonna be a great day!" as I headed out—those mornings when I had work—grateful to get to go clean another house or mow another lawn.

It wasn't until two years later in my journey that I learned that "mirror work" is actually a powerful healing tool recommended by many spiritual teachers. I first came across this teaching when my church book group was reading Louise Hay's *You Can Heal Your Life*. To rewire the "I'm not good enough" belief that most of us have deep within us, Louise recommended a daily practice of looking oneself right in the eyes, in the mirror, and saying one's name, followed by "I love you."

"Gabrielle, I love you."

This is what I had already been doing for two years, and I could testify to my book group about the life-changing power of this practice!

Letting Go of Limiting Beliefs

I also came to learn that the mirror work I was doing was part of a larger practice called "letting go of limiting beliefs." Limiting beliefs are the unhealthy, unhelpful thoughts we have picked up throughout our lives, often from well-meaning people like our parents, siblings, other family members, teachers, and religious leaders. One of the unhealthy thoughts I had picked up was that God would not approve of Gabrielle.

Fortunately, the ministers at my new church, Pastor Paul and Linda, taught that God created each of us to be the unique, beautiful individuals we are. According to this perspective, we actually dishonor God when we do not embrace our truths, because God is the one who made us as we are! That teaching, and the fact that the people at City of Light actually walked their talk and loved and accepted me for the trans woman I am, helped me let go of the limiting belief that transgender individuals are not pleasing to God. This allowed me to love myself at a much deeper level.

I remember having one particularly helpful talk with Linda, my pastor and new friend. For the weeks and months leading up to this conversation, I had been receiving accusatory texts from those from my old faith tradition. The gist of these texts was that I was deceived by Satan, sinning against my Creator, and displeasing to God. These accusations led to many sleepless nights where I wrestled with what I had been taught about God. And like the biblical character Jacob, who wrestled with an angel, I was determined not to let go until I had some answers!

Those answers came when I shared these accusations—and my own doubts and questions—with Linda. She responded, "Gabrielle, God knew you in your mother's womb before you were born, and before you were born, you were set apart. God created you as who you are, in God's very image. You are fearfully and wonderfully made" (Jeremiah 1:5, Genesis 1:27, Psalm 139:13–16). When I heard these old familiar verses—scripture I had known since I was a child—a new awareness dawned in me. I realized that God does not live in the boxes of my youth. God is much bigger than my gender identity so God can handle this! I let go of my limiting beliefs and accepted that God does love me and that I am pleasing to God. (In 2016 Linda wrote a very helpful book on what the Bible says in support of gender diverse people. See "Recommended Reading" at the back of this book.)

This was a radical shift for me, a truly life-changing conversation. Yet, I had also learned from Pastor Paul and Linda that it wasn't enough just to become aware of my old, limiting beliefs and release them once. I actually needed to take steps to create new wiring in my brain so it would start thinking these new, healthier thoughts, instead of simply defaulting to my old limiting beliefs. My ministers, as well as authors I have read, likened this process of rewiring my brain to reprogramming a computer. They called the thoughts of our new, healthier programming "affirmations" and encouraged all of us in the congregation to write and speak affirmations—the new truths of our lives—daily. So my new insights became my daily mantra:

> "God does not live in the boxes of my youth.
> God is much bigger than my gender identity.
> God loves me. I am pleasing to God."

I recognized that, for me, looking in the mirror every day and telling myself, "Gabrielle, I love you," had also been a powerful affirmation, a self-love affirmation. Linda pointed out that, even though I had picked up some negative perceptions about God's view of trans people in the faith tradition of my childhood, I had also learned some very positive affirmations. Only back in the day we had called it "memorizing Bible verses," not "saying affirmations." To this day, I still repeat to myself many of those affirmative verses, texts like "I can do all things through Christ who strengthens me" (Philippians 4:13) and "I am fearfully and wonderfully made" (Psalm 139:14). As you can imagine, some of these verses have taken on new meaning for me as I have embraced the truth of my feminine essence!

From Self-Love to Self-Acceptance

In spite of the mirror work I did and the affirmations I repeated, some days were just harder than others. Sometimes I would be at a restaurant, or in line for a movie, and I would catch people staring at my 6'3" frame and then turning to whisper and laugh at me with their friends. Those were some of the harder days . . . and there were many of them. Transitioning from being someone who was looked up to and respected to someone who was gawked at and made fun of was tough.

Just a few years into my transition, when I was really struggling to affirm self-love in the midst of society's frequent ridicule, I saw an interview with one of my "sheroes," Laverne Cox. Laverne is a tall, gorgeous, trans actress and advocate who rose to fame in 2013 playing a transgender character in the Netflix hit series *Orange Is the New Black*. In 2014, this rock star was featured on the cover of *Time* when the magazine did an article titled "The Transgender Tipping Point." During the interview I saw, Laverne shared how, even with all this fame and notoriety, she still got called derogatory names. Just walking down the street, trouble-makers would recognize she was trans and call out, "He/she!" and other insults. These experiences made her realize that she may never be seen as "just another woman"—that she might always be perceived as "different." Consequently, Laverne shared how she had to get to the point of being all right with being different, with being not just a beautiful woman, but a beautiful trans woman.

Seeing this interview was life-changing for me; it took my experiences with self-love to a whole other level. It empowered me to accept that I, too, am different—that I, too, am a beautiful trans woman. But that deep acceptance didn't come right away. I had to do more affirmations and more mirror work! After hearing this interview, I started looking into my mirror and saying, "Gabrielle, it's okay to be a trans woman. It's okay to be different. My uniqueness is beautiful." I kept saying these things over and over, every day, and sinking into the feeling of self-acceptance, until I finally believed these truths.

Acting on My Heart's Desires

Another segment of my self-love journey involved not just listening to my heart, but acting on its desires. In chapter 1, I shared the five things Dr. Paula Reeves identifies as the languages through which our hearts speak: our attractions, feelings, intuitions, dreams, and physical symptoms. Throughout my life, I had also heard people say that it is important to follow our heart's desires. Chances are you've heard this conventional wisdom as well. Personally, I have come to experience my heart's desires as a combination of my attractions and my feelings—a type of hybrid language—through which my heart also speaks. For example, the more joy and contentment I felt from finally living my life as a woman, the more I became interested in—that is, attracted to—the stories my trans friends told about pursuing surgeries and legal name changes. I soon recognized these growing feelings and this new attraction as expressions of my heart's desire to get my legal documents and my body more aligned with who I knew myself to be.

This process of aligning my external and public life with my internal knowing of my gender is called transitioning. There are three aspects of the transitioning process: social, legal, and physical. The things I have shared about my transition up to this point are parts of social transitioning: dressing differently, wearing a new hair style, embracing different mannerisms, going by a new name and pronouns, and coming out to my family and friends. Social transitioning also involved the scary necessity of using public restrooms that now matched my gender identity, since I no longer felt safe in the men's room. Legal transitions involve legally changing one's name and perhaps one's gender marker, and updating one's documents (driver's license, passport, birth certificate, etc.) and accounts accordingly (banking, credit cards, insurance, etc.). Physical or medical transitions may involve taking hormone therapy to alter one's secondary sex characteristics and/or pursuing one or more of a wide array of gender-affirming surgeries.

Not all people who are trans or nonbinary (individuals who identify as neither male nor female, or as a combination of both) choose to pursue all the different facets of the three aspects of transitioning. This is because some things may not resonate with our personal journeys or because we do not have the financial resources to make the desired changes. This lack of resources is exacerbated by the fact that many health insurance plans still do not offer transition-related coverage. Consequently, out of the 27,715 trans and nonbinary people who responded to the *2015 U.S. Trans Survey*, only 25 percent of us had actually had any of the various gender affirmation surgeries that are available. While 78 percent of respondents had wanted to be on hormone therapy, only 49 percent of us had been able to obtain hormones. The fact that some states do not allow us to make any legal changes prior to pursuing physical aspects of transitioning contributes to the reality that only 51 percent of respondents had a legal ID that reflected our chosen name. Likewise, only 33 percent of us had documents that reflected our aligned gender marker (the M, F, or, in some states, X for other, that indicates one's gender).[4]

The first three years of my transition had been taken up with pursuing the social aspects of transitioning: dressing as a woman, acquiring a whole new wardrobe, learning how to apply makeup and do my hair, embracing feminine mannerisms, choosing a new name, using women's restrooms, and coming out to my family and friends. My experiences during those initial years calmed my earlier fears and uncertainties. The reaction I had upon learning about the existence of trans people—"I could never live my life as a woman!"—gave way to thoughts of, "I *can* do this. I *must* do this. This is who I *am*!" By 2013, my heart's desires were speaking to me loud and clear: I wanted to have a body and legal documents that more accurately reflected my gender identity.

During that year I became good friends with Danielle, a trans woman who had completed all the legal and physical aspects of transitioning that resonated with her journey. Danielle graciously walked me through the forms and red tape involved in applying for a legal name change. It was an arduous process. After filling out the forms, I paid for an ad in the newspaper that had to run for thirty days, announcing to the world my intention to change my name. Once those days passed with no one coming forward to challenge my name change, a court date was set. I would have to appear before a judge to formally request a legal name change. The thought of making this court appearance was nerve-wracking. In 2013, many Americans still had limited knowledge of trans people, and I would be making my request in the South, in the state of Georgia—which has a reputation for being very conservative, both politically and religiously. My trans friends told stories of judges who had flat out refused to grant a legal name change to people like us.

These worries about the bureaucratic challenges were compounded by my own angst about taking a name that further separated me from my family of origin and my immediate family. Please understand that it was not my intent to disown my heritage or the name I shared with my wife and children. But many of my loved ones were not yet out about having a trans family member. In order to protect them, I thought it would be best to take a different last name, since we all still lived in the same metro area. Attempting to create a win/win/win that would allow me to honor my heritage, protect my family's identity, and be in integrity with who I knew myself to be, I kept my initials, GEC, but changed my three names. (In case you missed it, see the story of how I chose my names in the introduction.)

September 21, 2013, dawned bright and beautiful in Atlanta. As I dressed that warm, sunny morning, I looked at myself in my mirrored closet doors and thought, "Today I will officially be Gabrielle Elena Claiborne." I was so excited—and so apprehensive—all at the same time! How would things go? Would the judge deny or grant my request? My stomach fluttered with nervous excitement.

Danielle came to get me and drove us to the courthouse. Linda joined us there, for extra moral support. I remember sitting in the back of the courtroom and the judge calling me up. Despite my butterflies, I tried to look calm and confident as I approached his bench—standing 6'8" in my five-inch heels. The judge read my request, then looked at me.

"Is it your intention to legally change your name today, Ms. Claiborne?"

Heartened by his use of my chosen name, I courageously affirmed, "It is, Your Honor."

"Then by the power invested in me by the State of Georgia, I grant this request. Your name is legally changed."

Immediately my fears vanished! I felt exuberant! After thanking the judge, I rushed back to my seat to be greeted by my friends' welcoming hugs. The only thing bigger than the grins on Danielle's and Linda's faces was the thousand-watt smile lighting up my own.

After hushed congratulations were exchanged in the courtroom, Danielle guided me downstairs to the clerk's office. There I purchased ten beautiful documents showing my new legal name. By the time we got to the parking lot I could no longer contain myself. Free from the formal constraints of the courthouse I shouted to the world, "I'm finally me!"

From the courthouse, we immediately drove to the DMV to get my driver's license aligned. Then it was off to the bank to secure a debit card with my new name. At the end of a celebratory lunch, I was overcome with joy and relief as I handed that new card to our server. Never again would I have to endure the awkward stares of someone puzzling over how my feminine gender expression connected with a male name. Never again would I experience the anxiety caused by having to explain to TSA officers why the woman standing in front of them had male identification. Having these legally aligned documents took my feelings of happiness and contentment to a whole new level. Acting on my heart's desires allowed me to feel even greater alignment, which led to an even deeper experience of self-love.

As I was in the process of aligning my legal documents, I decided to act on another heart's desire and embark on a third aspect of transitioning: aligning my body with my gender identity. Trans women and nonbinary people desiring a more feminine gender expression usually start this process by starting hormone therapy, since the testosterone blockers and estrogen supplements we take will cause some growth in the breast area, along with other changes. But I was too eager to wait! Ever since I was a child, coveting my babysitter's bosom, I had wanted breasts. The breast forms Ramona gave me had been a satisfying start, but they were heavy and hot and they slipped around in my bra. After three years of wearing them, I was ready for the real thing!

Again, Danielle offered her support—and became a shining example of how people with resources can use their gifts not only for their own well-being, but also to improve the lives of others. Knowing my heart's desire and the financial challenges I was experiencing as I grew my three companies, Danielle put down the full amount required up front for my surgery, saying I could pay her back in small, interest-free installments. Without her generosity, there is no way I could have pursued a breast augmentation at that time. Danielle also connected me to a local cosmetic surgeon who had a reputation for working respectfully with trans women. After my initial consultation, a surgery date was set for several months out.

I soon discovered that the pendulum swings between excitement and apprehension I experienced before my name change had been mild compared to what I was now feeling with a breast enhancement date on the calendar! Even more than changing my name, having surgery felt like a point of no return. In the recesses of my mind I always knew I could change my name back; once I changed my body, there would be no going back. I cannot tell you how many times I asked Linda, "Am I doing the right thing?" And each time she would help me detach from the worries in my head and listen to the truth of my heart.

One time, when I was feeling particularly anxious, I remember her saying, "Gabrielle, I want you to take a few deep breaths and try to relax. Keep breathing deeply, and picture yourself three years from now. How will you feel if you're still wearing breast forms?"

My spirit deflated and I felt a great heaviness in my being.

Seeing those emotions cloud my face, Linda asked, "And how will you feel, three years from now, if you have your own breasts?"

Immediately my energy shifted as feelings of happiness and contentedness washed over me.

"So," Linda asked, "Are you doing the right thing?"

And I knew my answer.

And it was the right answer . . . because it was my heart's answer. Never once have I regretted the surgery I had on October 22, 2013. Six months later, I started hormone therapy, and I have never regretted that decision either.

Along with having no regrets, I also have no end of gratitude to Danielle and to the Health Initiative, an Atlanta agency that provided funding for the blood work I had to have to prepare for hormone therapy. While I was extremely fortunate to find financial support for aspects of my physical transition, I know that not all gender diverse individuals have access to such resources. But despite popular culture's fascination with our physical anatomy, being trans does not depend on whether or not we pursue any of the various aspects of physical transitioning. Being transgender is all about—and only about—knowing that our gender identity does not match the gender we were assigned at birth.

While pursuing physical aspects of transitioning did not make me transgender, I do acknowledge that having enough privilege to find the resources that enabled me to act on my heart's desires, and being able to muster the courage to push through my fears, were significant steps on my journey to self-love. And even though the desire to align your body and legal documents with your gender identity may not resonate with you, I am sure you can relate to my mixed feelings of excitement and anxiety as I contemplated making these changes. Perhaps you have experienced this emotional pendulum swing as you considered leaving a job to seek a better opportunity, or making changes in a relationship to create something more life-giving. While our heart's desires may be different, the feelings we work through to realize our desires are often the same.

·   ·   ·

In the beginning of this chapter I indicated that deepening into self-love has been a journey in and of itself. For me, the first leg of that journey involved simply looking in the mirror every day and telling myself, "Gabrielle, I love you." The next stage required letting go of limiting beliefs, of thoughts like, "God doesn't approve of me being trans." This letting-go process also required rewiring my brain by using affirmations. Another huge step in this journey was moving from self-love to a deep self-acceptance. This meant coming to fully accept myself as the unique and beautiful trans woman God created me to be. Then I had to act on my heart's desires and take milestone steps to achieve greater physical and legal alignment with my gender identity.

And the journey continues. Some days I find myself obsessing over body image, fretting about extra pounds I've gained or the wrinkles developing with the passing of time. On those days, I try to be gentle with myself and recognize these concerns as an invitation from my Creator to go deeper into self-love and acceptance. I anticipate new discoveries as I continue moving forward on this ever unfolding journey.

Your Turn
Embrace Your Truth Exercises #3 and #4
Mirror Work and Affirmations

If you desire to move forward on the journey of embracing your truth, I invite you to develop your own daily mirror work practice. Remember, this involves looking deeply into your eyes as you gaze into a mirror and saying, "(Your Name), I love you." And don't just say it once. Repeat it numerous times, deepening into the feeling each time you utter those powerful words. Some days you may want to switch it up a bit, and say what Louise Hay recommends in *You Can Heal Your Life*: "(Your Name), I love and accept you exactly as you are."

I also encourage you to reprogram your limiting beliefs by turning them into positive affirmations. Practice these affirmations daily as well. Of course, in order to do this, you first have to get in touch with your limiting beliefs. Here is something you can do to develop that awareness. Spoiler alert! Since this exercise builds on the "Your Turn" activity from chapter 1, I encourage you to complete that and not read any further until you do. The following exercise gives away some of the "secret sauce" of the first activity—which will be more effective if you're experiencing it without any preconceived notions.

In chapter 1, we learned that the people or things we are attracted to are often related to a part of our truth that is waiting to be brought forth and developed in us. It is also possible that we may have limiting beliefs blocking us from honoring these aspects of our truth. To get in touch with these limiting beliefs, consider the two things or activities you wrote down that you were attracted to, and choose the one that feels the most attractive to you. Now get a clean sheet of paper and write:

The reason I have not honored my attraction to _____ (fill in the blank with whatever you are attracted to) is _____

_____

Another reason I have not honored my attraction to _____ is _____

A third reason I have not honored my attraction to _____ is _____

A deeper reason I have not honored my attraction to _____ is _____

The bone-honest reason I have not honored my attraction to _____is _____

Now take a few deep breaths.

Determine which of the reasons yoiu listed has the most emotional charge to it, and let's turn that into a positive affirmation.

The most effective way to reprogram a limiting belief with a positive affirmation is by making your new affirmation the exact opposite of the old belief. The only exception to this rule is that you state your positive affirmation in the present tense. For example, suppose your limiting belief is, "I will never make money doing what I love." The exact opposite would be "I will make money doing what I love." But this statement affirms something that will happen in the future, and you do not want to wait until the future to make money; you want to make money now! So put your statement in the present tense by changing the word "will" to "now". This gives you the powerful affirmation, "I now make money doing what I love!"

Based on these instructions, I invite you to write your most emotionally charged limiting belief, as you determined above, as a present-tense, positive affirmation.

You can use your new, powerful affirmation in different ways. Writing it twenty to thirty times a day is a very effective way to reprogram your old limiting belief. You can also write your affirmation on sticky notes or 3x5 cards and put them in places where you will see them often—on the bathroom mirror and in your car, on your desk, and at the kitchen sink. Another powerful way to work with an affirmation is to combine it with your mirror work and say it while looking yourself in the eye.

Both of these powerful tools will help you remove blocks and barriers you may be experiencing and clear the way for you to continue on the journey of embracing your truth. You may also want to read Louise Hay's *You Can Heal Your Life* to learn even more about mirror work, using affirmations, and letting go of limiting beliefs.

Likewise, if you grew up in a faith tradition or a family that taught that it was selfish or wrong to act on your heart's desires, then you may need to let go of that limiting belief as well. To support you in this process, I recommend reading Edwene Gaines's

The Four Spiritual Laws of Prosperity. From this book I learned that all people can experience greater self-love by acting on their desires. Edwene wrote:

> (Accept) your desires. Don't be ashamed of what you want or feel that you shouldn't have the desires that you do. Your desires are holy. You didn't make them up. They were implanted in you by God. I mean, why would people who come from similar backgrounds desire such different things, if God didn't implant those desires in them?[5]

Because Edwene believes that our desires are God-given, she encourages her readers to set goals in order to realize their heart's desires. She then offers ten tips for acting on those goals. In one of these tips, she connects self-love with acting on our hearts desires by setting goals:

> The only thing we really have to keep in mind when setting goals is that God's highest law is love. God wants the best for us, always. With this in mind, why should we worry about anything else? Our job is to learn to love ourselves as God loves us. Only then can we truly love our neighbors.[6]

I wish you well as you continue on the journey of deepening your self-love, and thus your love for others, by acting on the desires of your heart.

FOUR

Embrace Your Past

Facebook post—September 22, 2018

Today was another step toward reconciling my past for me. Today, with the support of my amazing friend David, I attended my forty-year high school reunion. As we were driving to the event (which just so happened to be held at my old high school), I felt a knot in my stomach and a shortness of breath. After being reassured by David, "You got this, Gabrielle," we pulled into the school parking lot. To give some context as to just how significant the next few hours would be, the last time I was on this campus, I was a seventeen-year-old male who was the running back for the football team and high hurdler for the track team. As I walked in the door, the reality of being in a vaguely familiar place with people I hadn't seen in forty years both frightened and thrilled me.

I was about to connect the dots with a part of my past in a way that I had never imagined.

As I approached the check-in table a familiar face caught my eye. With a smile, she looked at me and said, "I know you. I'm so glad you came." At that moment, my heart grew three sizes. I took a cleansing breath and realized I was meant to be right where I was on that very day. Right before my very eyes, I was witnessing my past coming into alignment with my present. One by one, I reconnected with friends who were not only genuinely glad to see me but who were also interested in hearing my story. I even had an opportunity to chat with my ninety-year old principal!

Today was yet another reminder of the importance of showing up in the confidence of my truth with unwavering integrity. To the degree I do this, I will invite others to see and experience me as I want to be seen and remembered.

Many of us experience fears around showing up for class reunions, and that was certainly true for me, given my circumstances! That is why I am so grateful to my dear friend David, one of the newest members of my support system, for going with me that day to calm my nerves and bolster my courage. David is as wonderfully wise as he is incredibly handsome. Through his kind encouragement and warm congeniality he provided exactly the support I needed to help me reconcile a large part of my past with my present life.

This was a huge step for me because, in 2010, when I first came out as a trans woman, I was eager to put as much distance as possible between my past and my new life. I heard this same sentiment echoed by many trans people. While none of us wanted to lose our families or friends, many of us looked at almost everything else from our past as a mistake or an error. Some felt that way about their bodies. A few of my trans women friends felt that way about over-compensating in their career choices; they had pursued hyper-masculine vocations to "prove" they were men. Many of us had spent so much of our lives hoping to be free from our old persona that we wanted little to do with our former selves once we began embracing our true gender identities.

Three years into my journey, Linda noticed this disconnect in me. As my friend and pastor, she was concerned that I might not be able to love myself deeply in the present if I was hating my past. Linda invited me to consider my male years from a new perspective. She suggested that it might have been the experiences and characteristics of my old self that had actually enabled me to birth my new self. As we explored my past from this perspective, I began to see my life in a different light. Reframing things in this way helped me let go of the limiting belief that my past was a mistake and embrace it as the journey that had brought me to the place of being able to own my truth. Once I experienced this change in perspective, I became grateful for my past, and I felt much more alignment, peace, and self-love in the present.

For me, embracing my past involved much more than just mustering up the courage to attend a high school reunion. As is true for many of us, embracing my past also meant facing failures, disappointments, and unfulfilled dreams. This launched me on a journey of learning to forgive myself and others, a path that ran parallel to, and sometimes on the same track as the road to self-love.

Reframing My Past

In 2008, two years prior to my first appointment with Ramona, my male persona had the world by the tail. Three years earlier I had started a new owner's rep construction company and landed a contract on a $300 million project. The third year, as we completed that project, my company earned $1 million in revenue. This was my company's first million, and I felt invincible. My wife and I financed our older daughter's college education and our son's budding sports career, remodeled the house, and turned our backyard into a showplace with custom landscaping, a renovated deck, and a new entertainment area.

The month after completing that three-year construction project, my company was hit with a $1.5 million lawsuit. Unbeknownst to me, one of my employees had been embezzling funds from the project. Our client had discovered this and rightfully slapped my company with a lawsuit. I was appalled and outraged, and I felt like a failure—again. Armed with this new round of ammo, my Inner Accuser renewed their attack. "You should have known what your employee was up to! You should have discovered it, not your client! You're a terrible business owner—a total failure." To add to my feelings of shock, anger, and betrayal, I soon learned that I myself was being investigated by the FBI on charges of fraud conspiracy. For six tumultuous years the weight of this lawsuit and these charges hung over my head. Talk about sleepless nights!

The lawsuit and FBI investigation had been initiated in 2008, just as the national economy began to tank. All across the country, the construction industry skidded to a halt. Large companies laid off many of their employees and were able to ride out the storm. But small companies, like mine, folded one after the other. No matter how hard I hustled, I couldn't find another project, couldn't get another contract. My million-dollar company—which was now facing a $1.5 million lawsuit!—went out of business.

Months passed before I was able to find a job, no longer as my own boss, but working for another company. My wife went back to work and I gathered unemployment, but even these things did not keep us from having to borrow money from my parents. That was humiliating! I was a disappointment to myself, my wife, and the family. My Inner Accuser had a field day, constantly reminding me of all my failings.

Needless to say, these various failings were parts of my past from which I wanted to distance myself when I transitioned. But as Linda and I worked on reframing my past, I came to see how instrumental the pain of these, as well as other perceived failures, had been in my journey. Losing the company, enduring the lawsuit, and struggling to find work and make ends meet were what brought me to the precipice of "Enough!" I was well into my forties and had no idea if finding true happiness was a possibility. All I knew was that, up to this point, while I had known periods of satisfaction in my work and seasons of joy in my relationships, I had yet to find deep, lasting contentment in anything I had striven to accomplish.

A year prior to landing my $300 million contract, I had stumbled across the online pictures of trans women that gave me a vague clue about what was going on inside me. During the three years I worked out of state on that project, I bought lingerie online and wore breast forms and high heels in the privacy of the apartment I kept for work. While I longed to leave my apartment and experience life out in public as a woman, I was terrified by thoughts of "What would people think? Would I even be safe?!" I also had no idea where to even start with makeup, wigs, or women's dress sizes, so I settled for purchasing women's undergarments and wearing them behind locked doors. I will never forget the day I finished the project, packed up my apartment, and left that city. The last thing I did, before heading home to my family, was stuff all my new nighties, heels, breast forms, bras, and panties into trash bags and throw them in a dumpster. As I drove away, I could barely tear my eyes from the rearview mirror. It felt like my heart was being ripped out of my chest; it felt like I was leaving someone important behind.

Within a year, the anguish of leaving part of myself in another state, coupled with my failures and the pervasive lack of happiness in my life, ultimately brought me to the point of despair. I saw no way out, no way to escape the inevitable future of my life. I would forever be doing more of the same: working myself to death to keep up with cultural expectations, yet feeling like a failure—all while denying a feminine essence that was becoming more apparent to me.

For forty years I had struggled to repress my attraction to feminine things and make everyone else happy. When none of that worked, I finally asked myself, "What would happen if I stopped denying that still, small voice, and finally tried to find out what it is saying?"

True to the adage "When the student is ready, the teacher

will come," this was the point in my online research when I began seeing websites for dressing services. Thinking these services might help me discover the meaning of that still, small voice, I did the Google search that brought me to Ramona's Explore Your Feminine Side website. Seeing Gabrielle in Ramona's mirror for the very first time was the happiest I had been in a long, long time. That one moment of deep soul recognition—"That *is* me!"—propelled me forward on the journey of embracing my truth.

But I would have never experienced that life-changing moment if the pain of my failures had not brought me to rock bottom and challenged me to break through my fears of losing everything if I ever pursued my true gender identify. Once I realized the necessary part that pain and those failures had played in my journey, I was able to embrace my past in a new way. Shifting my perception—recognizing that all these bad things had not happened *to* me, but *for* me—led to deeper feelings of self-love, wholeness, and integration.

Feeling a sense of integration between my past and present was wonderful. It also felt great the day I was acquitted of all charges and the lawsuit against my company was dropped. But the anger and betrayal I felt regarding my embezzling employee (who was indicted and did serve jail time) was still there, along with the stinging shame of my failures. I knew I wanted to get to a point where looking back on my past would feel empowering and not debilitating. But I didn't know how to get there . . . yet.

Forgiving Others

About a year into reframing my past, the women's book group

Linda and I were co-leading at our church read Edwene Gaines's *The Four Spiritual Laws of Prosperity*. There I found life-changing teachings about forgiveness. Edwene wrote:

> An unwillingness to forgive is like stabbing our-selves with a knife and expecting the person who did us wrong to feel the pain. Forgiveness is not something we do for the sake of another person. *Forgiveness is something we do for ourselves.*
>
> Think of forgiveness as emotional house cleaning. It lets us make room for the good we desire. . . . *If we refuse to forgive, we are clinging to self-defeating feelings such as guilt, shame, blame, hurt, and resentment, and when we do this, we cannot feel truly worthy of having the best God can give us*; we cannot—and will not—accept God's gifts. . . .
>
> Forgiveness frees us from the endless loop of blame and bad feeling that keeps our minds focused on all the wrong things. *With forgiveness, we can let go of the past and turn to other, more important issues in our lives—such as how to be truly happy*, to have the things we want, and to thrive with a sense that we are joyfully fulfilling our life purpose.[7]

The idea that forgiveness is something we do for ourselves was new to me. Before reading this, I had thought that forgiving my embezzling employee would be the same as condoning his actions. But Edwene indicates that forgiveness in no way condones the wrong someone has done. It simply keeps us from poisoning ourselves with negative emotions.

Learning this enabled me to begin the process of forgiving my employee. Another thing that helped was learning from one of Linda's sermons that forgiveness is just that—a process. In fact, Linda defined forgiveness as *"the process of continually choosing to release negative thoughts and feelings about our own and others' harmful actions."* She pointed out that "choosing" is a mental process, not a feeling. This meant that forgiveness has to do with the thoughts we focus on, not the feelings we entertain. Consequently, every time I had an unpleasant thought about my employee, I chose to release it by not speaking it aloud and not continuing to rehash it over and over in my mind. Likewise, when something triggered my old feelings of anger and betrayal, I chose not to fuel those feelings by repeating, to myself or others, the story of how I had been wronged. Instead, when either negative thoughts or feelings arose, I mentally chose to repeat affirmations of forgiveness, and then I turned my focus to other, more life-giving things. After several years of practicing this forgiveness process, I finally got to a place where my negative feelings towards my former employee subsided; there was no longer a charge on any thoughts about him. I have since learned that this is how you know you have completed the forgiveness process—when you arrive at a place of emotional neutrality.

Forgiving Myself

Of course, it wasn't just my employee I had to forgive; it was my own failures, as well. Along with losing my company and failing to see the embezzling taking place, I also experienced failures within my family. Not being able to consistently provide for my wife and children was disappointing. But what were absolutely devastating were the two affairs I got involved in, long before I understood what was going on with my gender identity. More than any of my vocational failures, I felt the most guilt and regret over those mistakes. Despite my attempts to try to repair the harm I had done to our relationships, I was still haunted with remorse over the pain I had caused my wife and children. I wrestled constantly with the weight of knowing I had failed to be the strong, reliable husband and father they needed, deserved, and had once trusted. Continually beating myself up over the affairs seemed a just punishment for my mistakes. And without my even realizing it, self-flagellation took me down the slippery slope of knowing I had *done* a bad thing to the rock bottom of believing I *was* a bad thing: a lousy, unfit, flawed human being.

In *Daring Greatly*, author, researcher, and speaker Brené Brown writes, "The difference between shame and guilt is best understood as the difference between 'I am bad' and 'I did something bad.' Guilt = I did something bad. Shame = I am bad."[8] I had started out feeling guilty about my affairs; I was now bogged down in shame, as well.

It was from this gutter of guilt and shame that I began clawing my way to self-forgiveness. Upon hearing a Will Bowen quote, "Hurt people hurt people," I had an "Aha!" moment. It dawned on me that I myself had been hurting when I entered into the affairs. The source of that pain was my suppression and denial of my authentic self. Too scared to look within, I went looking outside myself for happiness. And, as often happens when we go looking for happiness in the wrong places, the results were devastating—for my wife, for my children, and for me.

A second "Aha!" moment occurred when Linda shared a saying she had coined, "We love to the limits of our wholeness." I realized I had entered into the affairs not only because I was hurting but also because I was broken. There is no way that I— or any of us, for that matter—can be whole while denying huge aspects of our essence, of our very being. Recognizing that a lack of wholeness impedes our ability to love in healthy ways, I now had a more accurate understanding of why I had done such hurtful things.

I still felt deep regret over the pain my family had suffered, but with these new insights, the burden of shame began to lift. I could now see that I was not a bad person; I was a good person who had done bad things out of my hurt and brokenness. From this new vantage point, I started to feel some compassion for myself. That compassion gave me the strength to crawl out of the gutter of guilt and shame and take my first wobbly steps on the path of self-forgiveness.

I received additional support for my self-forgiveness journey from other words of wisdom from Brené Brown. Along with addressing shame and guilt, in *Daring Greatly* Brené encourages readers to "speak to the shame" so as to "cut it off at the knees." She writes, "Shame hates having words wrapped around it. If we speak to shame it begins to wither. Just the way exposure to light is deadly for the darkness, language and story bring light to shame and destroy it." [9]

Prior to reading these words I had told only a handful of people about my affairs because I still had feelings of shame and embarrassment around them. This lingering emotional charge made me realize I had yet more work to do to fully forgive myself for these infidelities. Because of my great respect for Brené Brown's research and insights, I chose to try her shame antidote. During the summer of 2017 I was part of a book group composed of seven wise, caring friends. In one of our gatherings, with a quiver in my voice and tears in my eyes, I told them about my affairs. As Brené had predicted, speaking to the shame, bringing it into the loving light and presence of these supportive friends, did contribute to the ongoing dismantling of shame's power over me. I felt more peace and freedom than I had experienced in quite some time.

Nevertheless, the longer I live, the more I have come to know the path to self-forgiveness to be a long and winding road. I guess that's why I'm such a fan of the CBS show *Mom*. It focuses on the lives of two recovering alcoholics, Bonnie and her adult daughter Christy. The naked honesty with which this humorous sitcom often addresses the heavy topics of shame, guilt and forgiveness frequently reduces me to tears. I was especially touched by two episodes. One is an early episode where Bonnie, now several years sober, is trying to reconnect with Christy, who has just gotten sober. But Christy is having none of it. Even though Bonnie apologizes, asks for forgiveness, and demonstrates that she's changed, all her daughter can remember are the many times her mom has disappointed and neglected and hurt and humiliated her through-out her childhood. At one point Christy lashes out with, "You can't just waltz in here and say you're sorry and expect everything to be okay. It doesn't work that way."[10] And I've realized that, just because I've apologized and I've changed, that hasn't made every-thing okay for my wife and children. And I have to live with the consequences of that.

The other episode I could really relate to was a holiday show in which Christy, without malice, was laughingly sharing stories of all the times and ways her mom had ruined their Christmas celebrations. At first, Bonnie joins in the laughter, but then she gets up and leaves the room. Later, Bonnie tells her sponsor, Marjorie, that while those stories never bothered her before, this time she was overcome with remorse.

"Why am I feeling such shame and regret now, when I've never felt that in the past?"

Marjorie asks, "How many years sober are you?"

"Five."

"Then it's not surprising this is hitting you now. Look, I did so many bad things in my past and hurt so many people that, even twenty years sober, things are still coming up for me. This thing is like an onion. There's so many layers to it that we don't experi-ence them all at once. And that's a blessing. If we had to process the horror and regret of all the terrible things we've done all at one time, we'd overload. So you just got to take it one day at a time and keep doing the work whenever something comes up."[11]

And I'm finding this is true for me, as well. Even now, twenty years after those painful affairs, things still trigger new layers of regret and remorse, and I have to keep working at forgiving myself and making amends. And I've no doubt that things still happen that reactivate my family's hurt and pain. As Christy told her mom, "Just saying you're sorry doesn't get you a 'get out of jail free' card." My apologies don't take away my wife's and children's suffering, even though I so deeply wish they could.

In the midst of all of this, one thing that gives me hope, for myself and for my family, is the way that early episode of Mom ends. In the same way that Bonnie is working to reconnect with Christy, Christy herself, newly sober, is beginning to work the twelve steps. Christy recognizes that, in her drunken days, she failed her own daughter Violet in many ways, so she now asks her teenager for forgiveness. Of course, her daughter is no more willing to forgive Christy than Christy is to forgive her own mother. In the final scene, Violet yells at Christy, "Why should I forgive you when you won't forgive Grandma?!"

A stricken look appears on Christy's face as the truth of her daughter's words sink in. After several moments of charged silence, Christy slowly takes out her phone, calls Bonnie and, staring straight at her own daughter, says, "Mom, I forgive you."[12]

Of course, this is only the beginning. As I have already shared, in subsequent episodes Christy and Bonnie continue to experience triggers to their pain and remorse, and they have to continue working through the forgiveness process, from both sides: Bonnie continuing to forgive herself and Christy continuing to forgive her mom. Sometimes it's two steps forward and one step back. But they do keep moving forward, however slowly, and that gives me hope.

I have to confess, this has been the hardest part of this book to write and a section I would gladly have omitted. But I know that I am not the only person who has done hurtful things. I also know that self-forgiveness is an absolutely essential part of embracing our past. So I share my humiliating shortcomings and painful struggles in hopes that, if you can relate, you might find some support and encouragement for your own journey here. The path to self-forgiveness is indeed a very long and winding road, but if we share with each other what we know of the way, maybe we can all move forward together.

Meanwhile, in the midst of forgiving my employee and continuing on the journey of breaking free from shame and forgiving myself, I ended up experiencing another invaluable dimension of forgiveness. As someone who had been raised on the Bible—on a book that has a lot to say about forgiveness—I was surprised to discover I still had so much to learn!

Another Dimension of Forgiveness

"You *have* to go to this workshop!"

It was January of 2016, and my new friend, Joanie, was not taking "No" for an answer. She convinced me to attend the Loving Relationships Training, a powerful weekend workshop where we looked at all the relationships in our lives—our relationships with ourselves, our significant others, our family of origin, co-workers, God, money, and everything else!

That weekend, I had an epiphany regarding my mom. One of the trainers shared that, while our parents did the best they could for us, it may not have been all we wanted or needed. As a child, I had felt hurt because, while I had a great mom, she had not shown me the physical affection I deeply desired. She seldom hugged me or patted me on the back or tousled my hair. Based on what the workshop leaders had said, for the first time, I realized my mom's shortcoming had more to do with her than with me. Recognizing that my mother had done the best she could as a parent brought up feelings of compassion toward her. I began letting go of that hurt and, once again, started practicing the forgiveness process.

But this time, I experienced something new. Along with recognizing the need to forgive my mother, I also realized that, as a child, I had created an explanation for why Mom didn't show me affection; I had innocently believed it was because I'm not good enough. The workshop leaders explained how thoughts like these——beliefs we develop as innocent young children—can lodge in our unconscious. These unconscious thoughts then undermine our lives until we finally become aware of them, forgive ourselves for creating them, and rewire our thinking.

As I looked back over my life, I could see how the unconscious belief that "I'm not good enough" had starred in many of my undertakings. It had been the abusive voice—my Inner Accuser—that made encore appearances after each perceived failure to taunt and condemn me. So, along with doing my forgiveness work, I began reprogramming my thinking with the affirmation "I am good enough." To this day, whenever I am tempted to mentally beat myself up about some shortcoming, I still have to forgive myself, embrace my growing edges, and affirm, "I am good enough."

This experience taught me a critical dimension of the

forgiveness process. As we do our forgiveness work, it is vital that we ask ourselves, "What did I begin to believe—about myself, others, relationships, or how the world works—as a result of what happened? And is it true?" This last question, "Is it true?" is absolutely essential. Personally, I realized that many of the various beliefs I had developed were not true. For example, I am not a failure; I am not a bad person. It takes much work and great intentionality to reprogram these unhealthy beliefs, but it is worth it. Engaging in this vital dimension of the forgiveness process is a sure-fire way to unearth unhealthy, unconscious limiting beliefs so we can reprogram our thinking to create healthier, happier lives.

I have to confess, embracing my past and traveling the journey of forgiving myself and others has been extremely challenging. As I previously mentioned, it has required revealing shortcomings I would have rather kept hidden, and acknowledging painful experiences I would have rather ignored. But what I have come to know is that hiding parts of ourselves, repressing unpleasant emotions, running from our pasts, and being controlled by erroneous unconscious beliefs is a recipe for living a life of fear, anger, and painful physical symptoms. It leads to much unhappiness and actions we later regret. The only way out is to go within—to forgive ourselves and others, and to bring to light and reprogram our unconscious beliefs. At least this was true for me. According to the teachings of many spiritual and personal growth leaders, it is true for all of us as human beings.

Your Turn
Embrace Your Truth Exercise #5
A Forgiveness Template

If you sincerely want to embrace your truth, I encourage you to spend some time doing the hard work of embracing your past and learning to forgive. Because this work is challenging, you may want to seek the support of a spiritual leader, counselor, life coach, or very wise friend as you undertake it. Meanwhile, I offer you the following forgiveness template to use whenever strong feelings of ill will arise towards someone else—or yourself—based on something that has been done or left undone. (I include an example of how I used this template after it.)

In this moment I feel _____ and _____
and _____

While I honor and respect these feelings, I also choose to release these feelings along with the thought(s) that _____
_____
_____

I now choose to affirm that _____
_____

I also choose to think the higher thoughts that: Hurt people hurt others. If _____ had known better, _____ would have done better. I now choose to forgive _____

I now choose to bless _____ and wish them health, happiness, wholeness, love, joy, peace, and prosperity.

Here is an example of how I would use this forgiveness template when something triggered unpleasant feelings regarding the employee who embezzled funds from my company.

In this moment I feel hurt and angry and betrayed.

While I honor and respect these feelings, I also choose to release these feelings, along with the thought(s) that I'm not good enough and I am a failure.

I now choose to affirm that I am good enough and I am a success.

I also choose to think the higher thoughts that: Hurt people hurt others If my employee had known better, he would have done better. I now choose to forgive him.

I now choose to bless my employee and wish him health, happiness, wholeness, love, joy, peace, and prosperity.

When it comes to forgiveness, I found Edwene Gaines's book *The Four Spiritual Laws of Prosperity* and Brené Brown's *Daring Greatly* to be very helpful. Many other spiritual leaders and personal growth teachers have written about this topic as well. I encourage you to explore the abundance of resources available to support you in this vital practice of forgiving yourself and others.

FIVE

Persevere through Pushback

As we begin to embrace our truths more fully, we may experience pushback from others. Surprisingly, the source of that resistance is often those to whom we are closest—our family members and inner circle of friends—the very people from whom we typically expect to receive the most support.

A loved one's resistance should really come as no surprise. After all, those who are closest to us are the ones who are most invested in us staying the way we are. On some level, they know that if we change, then those changes may impact our relationship together; our change may lead to some adjustments on their part. And people are often resistant to change, especially changes they do not initiate. Besides, our loved ones liked us just the way we were. They were comfortable with how things were between us. Now we're evolving and they don't know what that means for them. However, people are often unaware that their discomfort with change may possibly result from their own fears and uncertainties. Consequently, when individuals are experiencing change that is coming to them from the outside, they may expend more energy pushing back against the perceived causes of that change than they spend processing their own fears. This is why we need to be prepared to persevere through pushback.

Be Prepared

One thing that helped me persevere through pushback was the fact that it did not take me by surprise. While I hoped my loved ones would eventually accept me for the person I truly am, I did not anticipate receiving their support when I first came out. That is why I took steps to prepare for pushback. As I shared in chapter 2, I created a support system for myself by reaching out to new friends and by connecting with a trans welcoming faith community. I made other living arrangements so I would have a space to explore my gender identity, a place where I was free to dress and live as Gabrielle whenever I was not at work.

The old saying is true: forewarned is forearmed. Think carefully about the changes others may experience in their lives as you embrace new aspects of your truth. Remember: the greater the changes, the greater the potential for pushback. Then prepare accordingly.

Step Away or Hold Space?

For me, as for many others in the trans community, exploring our true gender identity resulted in rifts between us and our family and friends. On Facebook, I would often see trans friends sharing their grief and disappointment over loved ones who did not accept and support them. Many times those posts would end with the heart-wrenching question, "What should I do?" Some responded by encouraging the writer to sever ties with the unsupportive person in order to protect themselves. Others recommended the path of forgiveness.

As I pondered how to handle all this, I recognized there are certainly times when someone's pushback can be so toxic or violent that a person must, for their own safety and well-being, step away from a relationship, at least for a season. However, feeling like I was not at that point with any of my family or friends, I decided I would commit to holding space for my loved ones. I recognized that my growth was resulting in changes in their lives, changes they did not ask for, did not want, and never saw coming. Given that I had been wrestling with accepting my gender identity for years, I felt it was only fair that I wait patiently, giving them space to have their own journeys with this change. I chose this course of action in an attempt to hold the door open for me to reconnect with my family members once they had some time to adjust to my new state of being—and to their new reality as it related to me.

I will be the first to admit that the path of holding space has not been an easy course to follow. There have been many ups and downs along the way, as illustrated by my experiences with my oldest daughter, Courtney. After my younger daughter insisted I tell her what was going on with me, and then coming out to my wife, I stalled on coming out to Courtney and my son. While I deeply regret this now, there were several reasons then why I failed to be proactive in telling my two oldest children. The main reason I delayed the discussions was my own fear of rejection. I was also trying to respect my wife's pleading admonitions not to tell these two, who were now in their early twenties, that I was transgender. In hindsight, I know my wife and I were doing the best we could at the time. We both feared, but were uncertain about, what my coming out to our two oldest might mean for them and for our family.

But again, one of my biggest regrets was not sharing my truth with them right away. I believe my stalling created stumbling blocks on their journey with my transition. While there is no way to go back now and undo what was done, I try to make amends by sharing my experiences and regrets. If you are an adult thinking of coming out to loved ones about your gender identity, I encourage you, if at all possible, to tell everyone in your immediate family at approximately the same time. If what you're sharing with them is something they may not have much knowledge or understanding about, try to provide resources they can use in order to learn more. (For coming out resources for LGBTQ people and their loved ones, please see "Recommended Reading" at the back of this book.)

As I mentioned in chapter 2, I also regret that I was not the one to actually tell my older daughter that I was transgender. In February of 2013, Courtney learned about my gender identity on Facebook. She immediately called me and said, "We've got to get together."

Fearing her reaction to Gabrielle, I went in my male persona to meet her at Starbucks. There, Courtney told me she wanted her dad back. She said if I was not willing to drop this charade, she would have no other choice than to have nothing to do with me.

I was devastated! All my life I had been the one to fix things for my kids; it had been my joy to make them happy. But that night, I didn't know what to say; I didn't know what to do to make things better. I felt as though I was letting Courtney down and betraying her, which were the last things I ever wanted to do. As we left each other that evening, I was afraid I might never see my daughter again.

Days . . . weeks . . . months . . . finally, a year passed with no communication from her. Because I was committed to holding space for Courtney, I periodically reached out to her via text and voice messages, but I never got a response.

On Father's Day of 2014 I was about to leave church when my phone rang. It was Courtney! She was outside and wanted to see me.

I panicked! Courtney had never seen Gabrielle in person. What was she going to think? What would she say? How would she react? All these questions raced through my mind—especially seeing as I was wearing a very short, very low cut dress that day!

After being reassured by friends that everything would be okay, I walked outside to meet her. As I rounded the corner, I saw Courtney standing by her car and smiling. I rushed to her. We embraced one another and I wept. I told her I loved her, and she said, "I just wanted to come wish you a Happy Father's Day." I interpreted this gesture as a welcome sign of progress.

After that, we began talking on the phone occasionally and we had a few dinner dates. During Christmas season of 2014,

Courtney requested that we spend some time together. Five years prior to that, 2009, was the last time I had shared any holiday time with a family member. When we met, Courtney told me she had been processing all this. She said she would always cherish the close father-daughter relationship we once shared, but she had come to accept that this relationship was over. As you can imagine, those words were a knife to my heart! But then she said something that revived me. Courtney said that now, despite the father-daughter form of our relationship ending, she was wanting to move forward with me, whatever that looked like.

"But in order for me to do this, I need you to answer a question for me."

"What? Anything!!"

She asked, "What do I call you?"

I didn't have an answer for her then, and we're still navigating the journey of coming up with something that works for all of us. But Courtney›s question gave me hope. It showed me she had really thought this through. She had contemplated numerous scenarios and had chosen to have me in her life. It's hard to express the tremendous relief I felt!

We had a lovely time together that afternoon. When I got home, I wept with joy and gratitude. I was grateful that my decision to hold space for Courtney had resulted in some reconciliation.

Yet, there have continued to be ups and downs in our journey. For many families with transgender members, milestone events like graduations, weddings, funerals, and even birthday parties take on an added layer of complexity. Who will be in attendance that doesn't know about the person's transition? If guests are learning about this for the first time at an event, will that take away from the day's primary focus, the joy or solemnity of the gathering? In light of such complexities, while Courtney accepted an invitation to join me for my birthday dinner in 2016, I was not invited to her wedding in 2017. I cried many tears over being excluded from that important day. As a parent, I always saw myself participating in my children's major life events, so to not be included was devastating. But my good friend Scott reminded me of the dynamic at play here. He said, "This is Courtney's special day and having you there would be just too much for her to handle." While this didn't make it any easier, Scott's wise counsel gave me a perspective I could embrace. It allowed me to work through the pain of not being there and renewed my hope that I could be included in future milestone events.

So goes the challenging journey of persevering through pushback by holding space. Sometimes it's two steps forward and one step back.

Selfish or Self-Honoring?

As we begin to embrace various facets of our truth, the pushback we receive may come in the form of questions like "Aren't you being selfish? Don't you care what this is doing to your loved ones?" These are accusations we must all be prepared to answer. Personally, I wrestled long and hard with these questions, and I came to understand that there is a significant difference between being *selfish* and being *self-honoring*.

Webster defines *selfish* as "concerned excessively or exclusively with oneself: seeking or concentrating on one's own advantage, pleasure, or well-being *without regard for others*" (*italics mine*). While some people accused me of acting selfishly, from my perspective, I did not. I was highly aware of the challenges my family and friends might experience in response to me living my truth—which is a big part of why it took me so many years to come out!

While I do not see my choice to live my truth as *selfish*, I do see it as *self-honoring*. I define self-honoring acts as those things we do in order to be in integrity with our authentic selves. I understand our authentic self to be the person whom God has created us to be. So for me, a self-honoring act is also a God-honoring act and thus, the best course of action I can take.

Yet I recognize and honor that others may take a different course. Within the trans community, there are stories of people who waited until their spouses or their parents died before they transitioned. That was the best way for them to live in their integrity. I also know people for whom the strain of knowing their truth, but not living it, became so great that they contemplated suicide. One trans woman finally asked her parents, "Would you rather have a living daughter or a dead son?" I firmly believe that each of us has our own journey to travel, and what works for one may not work for another. My decision to transition was validated early on in my journey by a comment made by my younger daughter. We were out for dinner, and she observed, "I've never seen you so happy or so at peace." For my daughter to recognize and comment on this was very meaningful to me. It made me realize that in order to bring the best I have to offer to my loved ones—and to the world—I first have to be my authentic self.

Over time, I also came to realize that I can only be as honest with others as I am being with myself. Consequently, in order to establish relationships that are based on the solid foundation of honesty and integrity, I have to be true to who I am; I have to be self-honoring. My life is a testimony to the fact that relationships based on self-denial are built on shaky foundations. And when those foundations crumble, rebuilding these relationships is extremely challenging. Yet, I am grateful for the chance I now have, with all those who knew me before I transitioned—and will allow me the opportunity—to establish connections that have a truer, more solid foundation.

Dealing with Internal Pushback: Letting Go of Guilt

Much of the pushback we receive will come from external sources. But there is also an internal source of pushback, and it comes from feelings of guilt. These are feelings that must be processed in order for us to continue successfully on our journeys of embracing our truth.

As I have shared previously, I had seen my living away from home prior to coming out to my family as a necessity. Over time, I learned they had experienced it as abandonment. This new awareness gave rise to deep feelings of guilt. My family means the world to me, so it was heartbreaking to know they had suffered such devastation in response to actions that had felt absolutely life-giving to me.

Working through my guilt was a two-step process. First, I had to forgive myself—again. This meant putting into practice all I had previously learned about forgiveness. I also reflected on a Maya

Angelou quote, "When we know better, we do better." This insight allowed me to extend compassion to myself and to acknowledge that I truly had done the best I knew how to do at that scary, uncertain time when I first began living as my true self. Unfortunately, my best had not been enough to create a win/win for me and my loved ones. Of course, forgiving myself wasn't something I had to do just once. No, whenever something triggered feelings of guilt I had to choose—and still have to choose—to forgive myself for my good-as-I-could-do but far-less-than-ideal actions.

The second phase of my process of letting go of guilt began in 2017. That was the summer I learned two important things from another Brené Brown bestseller, *Rising Strong*. In chapter 7, "The Brave and Brokenhearted," Brené discusses personal responsibility, expectations, disappointment, love, heartbreak, and grief. She illustrates these topics with several deeply moving stories. One account centers on the disappointment and heartbreak experienced by a woman dealing with her sister's alcoholism. Regardless of all the things this woman did to try to help her sister, the sibling continued in her addiction. From this story I learned that, no matter how much I wanted to take away the suffering my family members were experiencing in response to my transition, I could not. As the woman wanting to alleviate the suffering of her alcoholic sister learned, every individual is ultimately responsible for their own actions and responses.

Certainly this realization could seem indifferent and uncaring. It may sound like I'm saying, "Hey! None of my family's suffering is my fault! If they choose to be upset then that's on them, not me." But it wasn't like that—because my realization was tempered by something else I learned from that same chapter in Brené's book. This second insight came from things the author shares that hit so close to home they left me in tears. Brené writes about listening to a sermon given by her Episcopal priest in which he referenced a couple struggling to get to forgiveness following an affair. After talking about his experience of counseling this couple, the priest said, "In order for forgiveness to happen, something has to die. If you make a choice to forgive, you have to face into the pain. You simply have to hurt."[13] This made me recognize that, even if my family did get to forgiveness regarding their experience of abandonment, that won't take away their pain. They will still hurt.

Brené goes on to share the deep disappointments and intense grief she experienced in response to her parents' divorce, and her difficulties in owning all the emotions she felt as a result of the death of their marriage. She describes "losses that are more difficult to identify or describe . . . the loss of normality, the loss of what could be, the loss of what we thought we knew or understood about something or someone. Grief seems to create losses within us that reach beyond our awareness,"[14] making it even more difficult to process these losses—these deaths—that defy identification.

Knowing my family had experienced many of the same losses Brené describes broke my heart wide open. Her words invited me to acknowledge the deep pain and intensity of my loved ones' struggles. They allowed me to see how hard it may be for my family members to begin to name the multiple deaths they have suffered.

I also know that, while my loved ones may not be able to articulate all they have lost, they are still feeling these voids. This was brought home to me sharply through an incident my wife told me about. She was passing by my son's room when she noticed him sliding stuff under his bed. "What are you doing, Jason?" she asked.

"Nothing. Nothing," he replied.

Becoming curious, she stepped into his room and asked the question again. Receiving the same response as before, she grew concerned and continued to press.

Finally, Jason reached back under his bed and slowly pulled out several old photos that included me in my male persona.

With a catch in his voice, my thirty-year-old said, "I'm holding on to these so I don't forget what Dad used to look like."

Heart-wrenching incidents like this leave no doubt in my mind about the losses my family has experienced and the difficulty of the journey they are traveling.

In order to let go of the guilt that can arise in response to my loved one's pain, I have to cling to both of these things I learned from Brené: each individual's reactions are their own personal responsibility, and, while I cannot control another person's responses, I must honor and acknowledge the depth of their pain and their losses and struggles. For me, this means continuing to love my family deeply, even if, at times, I am only allowed to love them from a distance. It requires giving my loved ones all the time they need to work through everything that me embracing my truth is requiring them to process—even if this ends up being time in the afterlife, as may well be the case with my elderly parents.

I just have to say, letting go of guilt is not easy. In fact, it has been some of the most difficult work I have ever had—and still have—to do. In the process, I have learned that it requires exercising great compassion for myself and for others and truly knowing and believing, deep down, that we are all doing the best we can. For those of you for whom this is relevant, I encourage you to be kind and patient with both yourself and your loved ones. Commit to yourself that you will keep moving forward on the journey of continually choosing to persevere against guilt's internal pushback.

· · ·

We have now considered numerous things we can do to persevere against the pushback we may receive as we embrace each and every facet of our truth. Since "forewarned is fore-armed," we can begin by expecting it. This will prompt us to find new online or local individuals and/or groups to support us in our next season of growth. It may also require making new work and/or living arrangements. With those from whom we experience a great deal of pushback, we will need to decide whether to step back from those people, at least for a season, or try to hold space for them while they travel their own journeys in response to our changes. We may also need to think long and hard about how we will reply to the accusation that we're being selfish, all while exercising great self-care and compassion as we travel the journey of letting go of guilt. If there is some new facet of your truth that you are planning to embrace, may these insights help you persevere through pushback.

Your Turn
Embrace Your Truth Exercise #6
Prepare for Pushback

To help you prepare for pushback, I encourage you to write your answers to any of the following questions that feel relevant to your situation.

1. Which of my loved ones might experience the greatest impact in response to my embracing this new facet of my truth?

_____

_____

2. Is there anything I can do to lessen the impact of my changes on those who may be most affected by it?

_____

_____

3. If someone accuses me of "being selfish," how will I respond?

_____

_____

4. If I should lose a friend or family member's love and support, for a season or forever, how will I make peace with that? If I lose their financial support (if applicable), how will I deal with that?

_____

_____

SIX

Live Inside Out

2015 Facebook post

I've learned many important lessons in my journey of embracing my truth, although one stands out . . . one that I believe is generic to ALL of us REGARDLESS of our path of truth. It pertains to how we respond to those who come at us from a place of anger, judgement, abuse, or hatred. I've learned that these types of negative behaviors are birthed out of that person's fear that anything unlike me is wrong. Such responses originate from a place of uncertainty of one's own truth, thus requiring validation from others outside of themselves.

The fallacy in this logic is that no person's truth is based on someone else's perception. Rather, our truth lives within us. It is a unique reflection of God's creative essence—a unique reflection that is meant to shine in all its brilliance. So if I choose to react in retaliatory ways to life-depleting words and actions, then my truth diminishes, becoming something other than my own. I give away the power of my truth to others. Conversely, when I respond to such life-depleting attacks with love and understanding, my unshakeable truth then becomes a light and a source of encouragement, empowering others to embrace their OWN truth, in spite of all its perceived fears.

The question becomes, "Is my truth unshakeable?" What helps me determine this in my own life is evaluating how I respond to those who resist my truth. More times than not, this reveals the condition and reality of my truth . . . and sometimes it isn't pretty— YIKES!! But that's when I have to understand that my value and worth do not rely on external validation and endorsement; rather, they are a function of embracing the fullness of my truth in its creative, divine form. I KNOW when I'm operating in the fullness of my truth because validation from any other source other than from within isn›t a necessity. It is only THEN that my truth has set me free and LOVE HAS WON!!

. . .

I vividly remember the incident that prompted this Facebook post. Scott—the dear friend who rescued me from a volatile living situation and then let me crash on his sofa for three months—had moved to Florida. I was visiting him there for the first time, and we had a great weekend together. He had fun showing me his current locale, and I was a big hit with all his new friends. The icing on the cake was receiving the news, while I was there, that I had been named Atlanta's Best Trans Activist for 2015.

At the end of my upbeat visit, when Scott was driving me to the bus terminal, we stopped at Starbucks. While standing in line, the couple right in front of us turned around and stared at me for a longer than socially acceptable time. When they turned back and faced front, they began snickering and whispering to one another. As we waited for our lattes, they continued gawking at me and joking together. I got so agitated I finally spoke to them. "Can I help you? Is there something I need to know?" This was my way of showing them that their disrespect had not gone unnoticed; it was my way of trying to save my own self-respect. As often happens, when I actually speak to people who are making fun of me, this couple acted like they had no idea what I was talking about; they took no responsibility for their unkind actions.

When Scott and I returned to his car, he was silent for a few minutes. Turning to me with a puzzled, pained look on his face Scott said, "Gabrielle, I am so sorry that happened. I didn't realize you have to go through stuff like this. I thought everybody accepted you as the amazing, beautiful woman I know you to be."

I said, "Scott, I frequently have these sorts of encounters. They can happen any time I go out in public." He was shocked.

On the long bus ride home, I had eight hours to think about this painful, demoralizing episode—and others like it. I knew I didn't want to experience the hurt, anger, and emotional upheaval I frequently felt when something like this happened. I didn't want the rudeness and insensitivity of others to be ruining my days. The Facebook post at the beginning of this chapter was how I attempted to work through my thoughts and feelings as I journeyed home. Looking back now, I realize what I was trying to articulate here is what I have come to call "living inside out." Living inside out involves embracing our truths fiercely and living our truths courageously, without allowing others to impose their beliefs or expectations on us.

Up to this point, I have been sharing what we need to do to embrace our truths. Living inside out has to do with how we live our truths once we embrace them. I'm sure many of us have known people who have acknowledged some aspect of their truth, but they did not embrace it fiercely and live it courageously. Instead, they allowed the disapproval of others, or the challenges of their circumstances, to rob them of their joy. They became victims, not victors. I knew I did not want to live my life as a victim, focusing more on negativity than on the positive miracle of what I was birthing in my own life. And I'm sure you don't want to live that way either.

In order to live inside out, I had to find ways to amplify the whispers of my emerging truth, practices that empowered me to pump up the volume of my essence. As you read this chapter, I invite you to consider which of these tools you could use to cultivate the tender shoots of your own truth, so they can grow and blossom and produce fruit for the world.

Honoring Our Feelings

Like many of us, I was not taught how to honor my feelings. In fact, the conservative faith tradition I was raised in actually taught me that my feelings could not be trusted, that they were not a reliable basis for my actions. This early conditioning was reinforced by indoctrinating messages I received about being a guy. "Big boys don't cry" were popular song lyrics from my youth, and my football coach's playbook did not contain instructions for getting my ball of tangled emotions down the field and across the goal line of deeper self-understanding!

It wasn't until I was in my fifties that I came to a more accurate understanding of feelings and learned how to honor my own. The person responsible for much of my emotional education was Elizabeth Malone, the life coach I saw during 2014. You may recall that I met Elizabeth when she led the surprising "Get Your Sexy Back" workshop at the first women's retreat I ever attended. Sensing there was more I could learn from Elizabeth, I began seeing her for life coaching.

Inevitably, I would have some big emotional upset several days before my appointments. I would walk into our sessions an angry, frustrated mess. Elizabeth would listen to my account of the latest upheaval, then ask, "How do you feel about that?"

"I feel judged, rejected, misunderstood."

"Gabrielle, those are not feelings. Those are your thoughts, your perceptions of what someone is thinking about you. Get out of your head, and into your heart. How did this make you *feel*?"

With Elizabeth's coaching, I slowly disentangled from the angry tapes my head was running. As I listened deeper down, I heard other emotions playing beneath my anger, feelings like hurt and sadness. Once I got in touch with these emotions, Elizabeth helped me explore the source of these feelings, which were usually my perceptions that others were judging, devaluing, or misunderstanding me. Finally, Elizabeth would say, "These opinions that others may or may not have of you—are these your truth?" That is when I arrived at the point of owning that, despite what others may think or what mistakes I may have made, my truth is that I am worthy, I am capable, I am made in the very image of God, and I am enough.

Engaging in such explorations with Elizabeth, month after month, helped me learn that feelings are not unreliable things to be ignored. In fact, they are just the opposite! Feelings are an amplifier of truth, an internal GPS leading us unerringly to the innate beauty of our being. I simply had to get out of my head, look beyond my thoughts, invest the energy required to process my emotions, and follow the still, quiet voice of my heart. Each time I navigated this inner journey, I came home to the truth of my being.

As Elizabeth continued guiding me on these internal treks, I started learning the way on my own. When I encountered rude gawkers or other life-sucking situations, I began picking my way carefully over the rocky terrain of my feelings in order to arrive at my altar of truth. I soon discovered that each pilgrimage I made amplified my truth; I felt it become stronger, more unshakeable. And the more I visited this sacred place, the easier it became to find my way there again. I have come to the point now where I can usually process, within just a few hours, upsetting encounters that would have previously put me in a tizzy for days. This has saved much valuable time and energy, and has shown me, firsthand, the perks of living inside out.

Tools for Listening to Ourselves

April 15, 2013

This is the first entry in Gabrielle's journal. I feel so excited about this journaling journey I'm about to take as a woman. I hope it will allow me to understand and embrace my feminine essence the way God sees and intended me to be.

Every day I live, I feel more like a woman. When I look in the mirror, I see a soft, beautiful, mature woman. When I see her, I feel happy and on track with where she wants to go. Also, my heart is filled with joy that I have finally risked coming out.

Becoming a woman has meant a new relationship with God for me. I have been so concerned that I was not pleasing to God as a woman. I felt like God thought I was being disobedient and not a Christian. I worried I was being Gabrielle because of selfish reasons and not because this is who I am. But daily, Gabrielle is blessed with abundance, i.e., work, a compelling peace in my identity, endorsement from friends, and a passion for ministry to the marginalized. How do I interpret this? As God's destiny for me, or as my own selfish pursuit? I can't help but believe that my new identity is in perfect alignment with God's desire and plan for my life!

I feel God's pleasure as Gabrielle grows and develops into a woman. When the cares of this life seem so overwhelming, I recenter myself in my feminine energy and grace, allowing God to be my husband, my source of strength, my comfort. This is a new and refreshing perspective of God for me. It complements me as a woman. My hope is that I will see and experience God on a daily basis, allowing me to settle into my identity, find strength in my identity, and that I can give back to those who are searching and struggling with their journey.

This journal entry reveals that, three years after first stepping into the world as Gabrielle, I still had to listen very intentionally to hear the voice of my long-buried identity. Naysayers might think this is because I am trying to be something I am not; that my transition is unnatural. They would say I was born in a male body, so I should not be trying to live as a woman. But that's not why it had taken me several years to settle into my truth.

Unless you have lived in this culture as one gender and then lived in it as another, it is hard to fathom just how much gender impacts every single aspect of our being. As someone who's had to slough off fifty years of cultural conditioning about how I, a perceived-to-be male, was to live and move and be in this world, I can assure you, this is a journey that takes years! You have to relearn everything, starting with the small stuff—like that women chat with other women in restrooms . . . even with ladies they don't know! Men don't do that. For fifty years I had never spoken to anyone in a public restroom. Now I'm expected to make cocktail conversation while washing my hands and reapplying my lipstick! I know this sounds small and insignificant, but trust me, it took some getting used to.

And then there was the big stuff I had to relearn, like how to run a business as a woman. I knew all about being a male entrepre- neur. However, I quickly recognized that not only did my former masculine ways of conducting business not work well for others; they no longer felt authentic to me. But what style of leadership was right for me as a female business owner? It took time and trial and error to figure all this out.

I also had to relearn what it was to be a friend. Before I transitioned, my guy friends and I had engaged in side-by-side activities and talked about stuff going on outside of us. But as I was transitioning, I discovered that women sit down face to face and talk about what's going on inside them. And this is what my new female friends expected me to do! This was a huge shift for me—one I certainly welcomed, but that definitely required some adjustment! It also took time for me to feel comfortable sharing vulnerably and even more time to discern with whom it was safe to share so openly.

Because there was so much I had to relearn, three years into my transition, I still needed tools to help me amplify my truth so I could embrace it fiercely and live it courageously. For me, journaling became an invaluable tool for living inside out. Journaling gave me a specific time and space to engage in the absolutely necessary practice of turning away from the world's noisy clamor in order to listen deeply to the still, small voice within. It empowered me to pump up the volume on my truth so I could separate its messages from years of cultural yammering. I was not the sort of journaler who had a set time for writing each day. I just wrote whenever something was up for me or when I felt a need to connect more deeply with myself. And the more I listened to the truth speaking from my journal's pages, the more grounded and centered I felt.

Posting on Facebook became another way of listening to my truth. When I was going through the motions of living life as a man, I had no desire to be on Facebook. But stepping into my authenticity created a desire within me to connect with others. As you saw from the post at the beginning of this chapter, Facebook, like my journal, provided a place where I could observe and process the things going on in my life. This new practice offered the added benefit of allowing me to share my truth with my friends. I did this in hopes that they might be inspired by my insights, and I was always grateful when someone commented that what I wrote had been helpful to them.

My all-time favorite way to listen for my truth is spending a day at the beach. As a man, I had enjoyed many surfside vacations with my wife, children, and friends of our family. These had been busy, pleasant times of playing in the waves, building sand castles with the kids, and socializing with the adults. As a woman, I found myself having a very different experience of the beach. All I wanted to do was lie on the sand and bask in the sun. For reasons I couldn't quite articulate, I found this experience to be incredibly rejuvenating for me.

Three years into my transition, I convinced my friend Linda to take a relaxing beach vacation with me. I had to talk her into this because Linda is not one of those people who is comfortable just lounging around; she's always up doing something. But as the week progressed, she settled in and actually started enjoying our lazy days, even waxing philosophical:

> "I never realized how much the beach engages all five senses. I feel the silk of the sand, the warmth of the sun. I hear the waves and the gulls. I taste salt water from our swim and smell salt in the air. And all around us, I see water reaching for the horizon and clouds shifting across the sky. No wonder you like the beach so much, Gabrielle! The way it engages all five senses . . . it's the perfect mind-body-spirit cleanse!"

Linda's reflections helped me articulate what I now love about sun-drenched days at the beach. As the sound of the surf drowns the voices in my head and the heat of the day melts the tension from my body, I am left with a deep sense of connection to my truth; I bask in the knowing of my essence. As the sun fires my truth into a solid core, I am strengthened to live my life inside out.

Tools for Celebrating Ourselves

Over the course of my journey, I've discovered something else that empowers me to embrace my truth fiercely and live it courageously: doing the things I truly enjoy. For me, shopping, bubble baths, girls' night in or out, traveling, seeing a play, singing in the choir, sharing dinner with friends, being part of a book group, and volunteering in organizations whose missions resonate with my passions are all things that make me happy. Of course, after engaging in lots of activities, I also need time to chill by watching a Hallmark movie or a game—preferably hockey or college football. Making space for all that makes my heart sing—both the doing and the down time—grounds and centers me in the truth of my being.

In the world we live in, there are so many people and things telling us who we are and what we ought to be. Some of these sources have our best interests at heart; but not all of them do. That's why it's so important for each of us to learn to live in such a way that we don't allow others to impose their beliefs or expectations on us. Learning to honor my feelings, finding practices that help me really listen to my essence, and doing the things I love are what help me live my life fiercely and courageously. They are the practices that empower me to live inside out.

Your Turn
Embrace Your Truth Exercise #7
Amplify Your Truth

At the beginning of this chapter I invited you to see if any of the practices I use to amplify my truth resonated with you. Did they? Or do you have other things you do that strengthen your essence? I know some people find meditation, yoga, walks in nature, working out, or time spent with their pets to be practices that empower them to live inside out. The important thing is not *what* you do to amplify your truth; the important thing is to do *something*.

I encourage you to write down the practices you already do—and/or one you are willing to try—in order to embrace your truth fiercely and live it courageously. If you're having trouble thinking of things, try this: make a list of nine things you really like to do, nine things that make your heart sing. Write

- three things you loved doing in the past,

_____

_____

_____

- three things you really enjoy doing now, and

_____

_____

_____

• three things you've always wanted to do, but haven't done yet.

_____

_____

_____

Now pick one thing from your list and put a date beside that. Commit to doing it by scheduling it on your calendar.

After you do this one thing, further amplify your truth by writing about the experience or sharing it with someone. And don't just describe what you did; tell how it made you feel. Celebrate yourself by basking in this experience of doing your truth.

Then choose another thing from your list—and repeat the process!

SEVEN

Live Your Purpose

Our job is not to be Mother Teresa,
our job is not to be St. Francis
—it's to do what is ours to do . . .
Our first job is to see correctly who we are,
and then to act on it. That will probably take
more courage than to be Mother Teresa.
—Richard Rohr, *Everything Belongs*

The good news about embracing your truth is that it doesn't just make your life better; it also makes the world better. Denying any aspect of our truth takes energy. The energy we expend repressing our truth is energy we do not have to invest in our relationships, workplaces, spiritual communities, neighborhoods, and the rest of our world. We bring the greatest light to the world when we just shine with all the brilliance that is our true selves. Simply stated, the best way to "Bring it!" is to "Be it!"

Finding My Purpose

"Is there some particular reason why you wanted to see me—something specific you'd like to work on?" That was the question Elizabeth posed to me in our first life-coaching session.

"Yes. I'd like to find my life's purpose."

In the faith tradition I grew up in, people were always asking, "What's God's will for your life? Have you found your purpose yet?" These questions resonated deeply with my strong desire to make a difference in the world once I somehow, somewhere found God's will for my life. But in four decades of searching, I had never felt like I had found my true purpose.

Typically I would see Elizabeth once or twice a month, but, despite my stated goal, our conversations never focused on "My Life's Purpose." Instead, Elizabeth taught me how to listen to my feelings. She also coached me on trusting my intuition, another skill I had not learned from my football coach! Since our feelings and intuitions are two of the languages through which our hearts speak, learning to understand these languages enabled me to not only *listen* to my heart, but also to *act* from my heart. As I moved more and more into heartfelt action, slowly but surely, my life was becoming increasingly fulfilling.

About a year into working with Elizabeth, I finally had a session where, for once, I wasn't arriving in crisis mode; there was no burning issue that needed addressing. So Elizabeth suggested we spend our time reflecting over all that had transpired throughout that year of 2014. We talked about the progress I had made in learning to listen to my heart and the changes that had resulted from my heartfelt actions. We discussed positive things that were unfolding in my life—reconciliation with family members and new opportunities. Joining the Atlanta Gay and Lesbian Chamber of Commerce (now the OUT Georgia Business Alliance) had significantly increased the number of clients in my cleaning business. A friend and I were given the opportunity to co-host a radio show exploring topics of interest to the trans community. In the fall, I had volunteered at the Pride festival, co-chairing the VIP Committee. I was then invited to serve on the Board of Atlanta Pride, an amazing organization that was serious about creating more trans inclusion throughout its operations.

When I finished sharing all these new developments, Elizabeth said, "Wow, Gabrielle! Look how far you've come! Look at what you've accomplished! I see you making a differ-ence in the lives of everyone around you, just as you're going about your business each day, embracing your truth, and living your authentic life."

When Elizabeth said this, I suddenly had a new insight. I realized my life's purpose isn't some pot of gold at the end of the rainbow; it isn't about getting to some future destination. In fact, it turns out my purpose isn't something I had to find at all! As I embraced my truth fiercely and lived it courageously, *my purpose found me*. I now realized that what brought joy to my heart and light to the world was advocating for the trans community by doing whatever I could to support my trans siblings directly and by helping cisgender people understand gender diverse individuals.

131

Another 2014 opportunity gave me the idea that public speaking was to be the means through which I would do my advocacy work. During that year, my church began inviting one individual each Sunday to share what the congregation meant to them—how it had impacted their lives. I was honored when Pastor Paul asked me if I would be willing to do this—and also scared! Living as a guy, I had never felt right or comfortable speaking in front of large groups. But now, four years into embracing my truth, I was excited about this opportunity. The congregation had been so supportive of my transition—so instrumental in helping me explore and flourish in my true gender identity—that I wanted to share my gratitude with them. Still nervous about public speaking, I wrote out what I wanted to say and rehearsed it numerous times.

Things went great the Sunday morning I spoke. I felt like my heart was reaching out and connecting with every single person in the congregation. I knew I had found my sweet spot.

This internal knowing was confirmed by much positive feedback. One parishioner said, "Gabrielle, thank you so much for sharing from your heart. It means a lot to me to know what a difference I've made in your life, just by being part of this trans affirming congregation." Danielle, the friend who guided me through the physical and legal aspects of transitioning, said, "Girl, this is what you should be doing, right here." I felt the truth of these affirmations and was excited about new possibilities. But like many of us—especially when we are just beginning to recognize our purpose—I had no idea where to start.

Start Anywhere . . . and Have Fun!

"Let's brainstorm some possibilities!" This was my friend Linda's enthusiastic response when I shared my growing desire to advocate for the trans community through public speaking. I told her my goal was to inspire others to be their highest and best, while helping them understand gender diverse people. I also wanted my audiences to recognize that, as members of the human family, the things we have in common are much greater than our differences. Because Linda was a minister and I was a lifelong church leader, we decided to start by getting my message out to spiritual communities.

After tossing around various ideas, Linda volunteered to work with me to design and offer a personal growth workshop that actually became the framework for this book. The workshop gave people insights on how to embrace their own unique truths while using stories from my personal journey to illustrate each insight.

We hosted our first workshop on April 11, 2015—with just seven people in attendance! Participants offered encouraging praise for our content while kindly adding, "And we know your delivery will get better." Later that month, Linda and I were given an opportunity to share our workshop at the same "Harnessing Your Divine Feminine" retreat where I had met my life coach, Elizabeth. It just so happened that we were scheduled to be the first presenters on Saturday. But what neither we nor the retreat organizers knew was that the night before we did our presentation, ABC was set to air the final interview Caitlyn Jenner did before she transitioned. Many of us women on the retreat were among the approximately 17 million viewers of that iconic interview—

and it certainly primed the pump for all we shared the following morning! The synchronicity of those events felt like a little wink from God, affirming and encouraging my fledgling attempts to live my purpose.

After we held an August workshop for a small group of New Thought leaders, one participant came up to me with tears in her eyes. She said, "Gabrielle, my teenager recently came out as transgender, and I'm still calling them by their old name. I had no idea how life-giving it is for trans people to have their loved ones acknowledge their new names and pronouns. I'm committing to doing better at this."

That mother's comments validated my efforts on a whole new level. It was so life-affirming to hear that sharing my experiences could help a parent better support their trans child. In fact, I later learned that having their mother's support just might have saved this child's life. A 2012 report showed that, during the year prior to the study, 57 percent of trans youth ages 16–24 whose parent(s) were only somewhat or not very supportive of their gender transition had attempted suicide. However, the attempted suicide rate decreased significantly—to 4 percent—for youth who had supportive parent(s).[15] This experience also showed me the magnitude of a parent's journey with a transitioning child—the grieving they have to go through and all the adjustments they have to make. This firsthand awareness helped me have more patience with my own parents and renewed my hope that, one day, they too might find their way to acceptance.

In November, a colleague of ours, Rev. Diane Dougherty, orchestrated an invitation for us to speak at our first conference.

Linda and I travelled to Milwaukee for Call to Action, an annual gathering of Progressive Catholics. As a transgender advocate, I would have never guessed that the first large gathering I would present at would be a Catholic conference! A doctor who attended our session told me, "I have felt so uncomfortable with my trans patients, but now I know how to interact with them respectfully. Thanks so much for what you shared." A mom came up and said, "My six-year-old trans daughter is at the conference with me, and I want her to meet you. She needs role models." Again, these comments confirmed my hope that I could make a difference for trans individuals—and cisgender people who wanted to be supportive, but just didn't know how—by engaging in public speaking.

Although I hadn't known where to start, as a result of simply starting somewhere, things began to unfold. Becoming friends with more gay, lesbian, and bisexual individuals showed me that, although we're often referred to as the LGBT community, many LGB people actually know very little about the T—that is, about us trans folks. Serving on the Board of Atlanta Pride gave me the opportunity to attend regional Pride leadership conferences. Upon learning that these conferences welcomed workshop proposals, I created a seminar called "Making Your Pride Organization Trans Friendly." I had the privilege of facilitating this seminar at several regional conferences, and even at InterPride, the biennial gathering of global Pride leaders. The seminar received rave reviews and led to my being hired by several East Coast Pride organizations to do trainings for their leadership teams.

It is true that "practice makes perfect," and with every presentation, my delivery improved. Meanwhile, Linda and I decided we made a good team. To our advocacy work, I brought my lived experiences as a trans woman, an extrovert's love for networking, knowledge of the corporate world, and my entrepreneurial background. Along with her ministerial training, Linda brought her expertise in teaching, writing, research, and curriculum development. Since we were having fun working together, we continued to be intentional about expanding our reach. We hired a colleague from the OUT Georgia Business Alliance to create a website for our fledgling company, which we named Transformation Journeys Worldwide (TJWW). When my Atlanta Pride connections resulted in two corporate training engagements in the summer of 2016, we officially established TJWW as an LLC and opened a company bank account. We were on our way!

In *The Four Spiritual Laws of Prosperity*, Edwene Gaines writes:

> "Your divine purpose . . . doesn't have to be something huge or lofty or self-sacrificing. It just needs to bring you joy. . . . You start by doing, and then the world opens up a larger arena for you to play in, and eventually you move toward prosperity while you do it. . . . I believe that's how the process works."[16]

Author and career transition expert Tama Kieves shares her experience of this same process in *Thriving through Uncertainty*. She writes:

When I first left law, I felt the desire to write poems. "Oh, now we're talking," hissed my critical inner voice. "This is what we busted butt for in antitrust law, so that you could write about the geese?" But you don't get to choose what you love. It chooses you. And it's often just what comes before a comma, not a period.

For example, writing poetry led me to writing deeper essays about the journey of career transition, which turned into my first book, *This Time I Dance!* And as I wrote, I followed the intuition to start a support group, which led to teaching, which led to coaching, which led to putting on national retreats, which led to global programs online and more. . . . One thing led to another and another. This is the radical path of following bread crumbs to everything you want.[17]

Elsewhere in her book, Tama wrote, "We are not looking for answers, we are looking for next steps."[17] This was certainly true for me. When it comes to living your purpose, it doesn't matter where you start. Just start somewhere . . . and have fun!

Rising Strong

But of course, not every day will be fun.

"I bombed! I didn't even get through my whole speech when they called time, and I had to sit down. I failed! I blew it! I'm just going to crawl into this hotel bed and hide here until the conference is over."

Linda caught the full force of my anguish as I wailed my self-condemnation down the phone line connecting us from Indianapolis to Atlanta. This was the weekend I was presenting my "Making Your Pride Organization Trans Friendly" seminar at the conference for international Pride leaders. The presentation had gone great; my upset was related to a different endeavor.

At each InterPride conference there are elections to fill vacant board seats. That year there was an election for a trans-identified board member. At the eleventh hour, some of the East Coast Pride leaders who had previously hired me to train their local leadership teams encouraged me to run for the position. I was honored that they recommended me, and I was open to extending my trans advocacy work into a larger arena. I quickly submitted my application and credentials and began working on the two-minute speech each candidate would have an opportunity to present, on the Conference floor, just before attendees would vote to fill this vacancy.

This two-minute speech was what I had blown—and I lost the election. Although the vote was 46-54, by not getting through all I had rehearsed, not hitting my strongest credentials, I felt like I had failed myself and the Pride colleagues who had put their faith in me. Hot with shame and embarrassment, I escaped back to my hotel room, burrowed into the bed, and called Linda.

This was October of 2017. A few months prior, Linda and I had been part of a book group that discussed Brené Brown's bestseller *Rising Strong*. Referencing Theodore Roosevelt's 1910

"Man in the Arena" speech, Brené explores what it takes to get up and keep moving after we try and fall, when we find ourselves face down in the arena. This was certainly where I found myself on that October day. Linda pulled out all her pastoral skills—and some tough love—to get me out of that bed. "Gabrielle, this is exactly what we learned about in Brené's book. Yes, you've fallen; you risked expanding into a bigger arena, and now you're face down in that arena. But what will determine whether or not you fail in this situation is if you choose to stay in that bed, or if you rise strong and go back down to that conference floor, hold your head high, and continue being the warm, gracious, highly capable individual you are."

As much as I dreaded facing everyone again, I knew Linda was right. There's no shame in trying and falling; I only fail if I fall and stay down. So I pulled myself out of bed, dried my tears, reapplied makeup, and went down to the next plenary session. And people were very gracious. In stark contrast to my self-perception, no one so much as hinted that they thought I had bombed; instead, they thanked me for being willing to run. A weekend that could have ended in failure did not. In fact, I actually ended up enjoying the rest of the conference.

Later I was able to reflect on the lessons learned. I realized that, in my public speaking, I needed to trust my heart more and not worry so much about a script. This lesson has served me well as I expanded my speaking from training engagements to a TEDx Talk and keynote addresses. I also realized that, as I do new things in order to play in larger arenas, I'm not always going to do every-thing perfectly. There's going to be a learning curve. If I had let that one incident defeat me by defining me as an incompetent failure, then I would not be where I am today.

And I believe this is true for all of us. On the journey of living our purpose, a fall can be a detriment to our growth—or an invitation to our greatness. We can flop—and still fly. A fall can also be a needed lesson, a temporary setback, or a necessary pause. It is certainly a time to reach out to the support system we've built and seek our friends' wisdom and encouragement. A fall is not the same as a failure. A fall is an opportunity to rise strong and build resilience.

Create a Vacuum

Another lesson I have learned on my journey is that sometimes you must intentionally create a vacuum in order to make space to live your purpose. During 2015 and 2016, as Linda and I were launching Transformation Journeys Worldwide, I still had my cleaning company, the home renovation company, and my lawn care company. I had started all three back in 2012, when I first decided to embrace my truth fully and live 24/7 in my true gender identity. Because I was the primary employee in each of these companies, they required much of my time. Even when I was able to hire assistants, I still worked our jobs with them during the day. Meanwhile, I was also handling phone inquiries about my companies, squeezing in job site assessments at the mercy of potential new clients' schedules, and writing proposals for these opportunities in the evenings or over the weekends.

But as Transformation Journeys Worldwide began to grow, trying to juggle everything became increasingly challenging. Since the lawn care company had never gained much traction, it was easy to let that go. On the other hand, home renovations, being the most skilled services I offered, were also the most profitable. Yet, the more I settled into my feminine essence, the less I felt like swinging a hammer and cutting 2x4s. While I know many women who enjoy building and renovating, it turns out I am not one of them. Likewise, the heavy toolbox I had easily toted prior to starting hormone therapy became difficult to lug as the testosterone blockers and estrogen supplements made their anticipated changes in my body. While I loved the softening of my skin and the slight curves the hormones were creating in my figure, the loss of muscle mass and physical strength—although equally predictable—were not welcome effects. By the end of 2016, I decided to let the home renovation company go. I chose to honor the growing feeling that it no longer resonated with the truth of my being and to intentionally create more space for speaking engagements.

As time went on, Linda and I learned about local corporate networking opportunities. We also recognized that it was important that I show up at these events. Linda is a 5'2" introvert, but I have the extrovert's natural ease and enjoyment of meeting new people and learning what they do. Linda often tells me that I am our company's best business card. She says, "Gabrielle, people remember a gorgeous, 6'3" trans woman—especially when you're standing 6'8" in those five-inch heels you love to wear!"

Showing up at these networking events, along with my board service with Atlanta Pride and my membership in the OUT Georgia Business Alliance, led to invitations to do "Trans 101" trainings—often for corporate LGBTQ employee or business resource groups. Most of these training opportunities were "Lunch and Learns"—and many of the networking events also took place during the middle of the business day. Since it takes me a good two hours to become that "gorgeous 6'3" trans woman"—what with the time required to shower, dress, and do my hair and makeup— it became increasingly difficult to schedule my cleaning clients around our TJWW opportunities.

By mid-2017, Linda and I began talking more about the possibility of me letting the cleaning company go so I could come on full-time with Transformation Journeys Worldwide. Since we did not yet have the volume of work to support both of us full-time, we knew it would be a leap of faith. By this point, we had become familiar with the spiritual teaching that if you want to invite more good into your life, you first have to create a vacuum by letting go of what no longer serves you. While my cleaning company had served me well, providing me a way to financially support myself when I first transitioned, more and more it was feeling like it was no longer mine to do. As if to encourage me to take this leap of faith, I began experiencing invitations from God, from the universe—from whomever you feel comfortable attributing them—to take this next scary step. One of my long-time clients let me know they would soon be discontinuing my services because they were moving out of state. My one commercial client told me the organization had to tighten its budget and find ways to cover its cleaning needs in-house.

The thought of letting go of the company that provided my financial security terrified me. But I also recognized that working in it no longer fed my soul. While I had once taken pride, as a trans woman, in building this business from the ground up, now . . . it just felt like work. Meanwhile, the more training and motivational speaking I did, the more I felt aligned with my purpose. Advocating through public speaking fed me, resonated with me, affirmed me. This was now what was mine to do.

By October of 2017, I decided to step out in faith and go full-time with Transformation Journeys Worldwide. Throughout this decision-making process, along with my own personal fears, I had also been struggling with worries about the trans employee who had been faithfully working with me in the cleaning company for more than two years—I didn't want to leave her jobless—and with concerns about my clients. I felt bad about discontinuing services to people who had become my friends and whose support had been instrumental in my journey. Both of these issues resolved themselves when my employee decided to take over the company and continue offering its services. This taught me another lesson about the importance of living my purpose. It made me realize that when I am not doing what is mine to do—if I'm doing something out of fear, obligation, or just to get by—it takes away an opportunity for others to step into their greatness and do what is theirs to do. If I had not left my cleaning company, my employee may never have stepped up to live more fully into her purpose by becoming a business owner.

Now, I wish I could say—and I'm sure you probably want to hear—that as soon as I came on full-time with Transformation Journeys Worldwide our phone started ringing off the hook and we had more engagements than we could handle. But that's not what happened. On the contrary, those first few years were pretty lean.

But Linda and I kept on keepin' on. We continued to show up. And slowly but steadily, our company, and the range of services we offer, has continued to grow.

I hear similar stories from other people I know. Living your purpose doesn't necessarily make you an overnight success. But it does allow you to go to sleep each night content in knowing that you are living in your authenticity, making a difference in the world, and doing what is yours to do. For me, this has been a source of deep and abiding joy, and I wish the same for you.

Your Turn
Embrace Your Truth Exercise # 8
Discover Your Purpose

In order to live your purpose, you first have to find your purpose, or let your purpose find you. Once you recognize what is yours to do, you can begin by simply starting anywhere, although you may need to create a vacuum—to let go of activities that no longer serve you well—in order to free up time to pursue your passions. To help move you forward with this aspect of embracing your truth, you may want to write answers to the following questions.

1. What are things you do, or things you have done in the past, that really make your heart sing, that give you a deep feeling of contentment? Don't worry that it's not important enough or not significant enough. Don't worry about what any of it means. You'll figure that out later. Just write everything you think of, as quickly as you can . . . and have fun with this!

_____

_____

2. What are activities you must have in your life, or abilities you must use, for your own well-being? What are the things or skills that, if missing from your life—if you couldn't do or utilize them—you would feel like a part of you was also missing?

_____

_____

3. Are there any causes you feel passionate about, perhaps because they have impacted your life in some way? If there are not, what is something you see that needs doing in this world that requires the kinds of skills you like using and the sorts of things you like doing?

_____

_____

4. What are some vocational and/or volunteer opportunities where you could use the skills you identified in answer #2? And how might you use the things you said you like to do in answer #1 in service to the cause or thing that needs doing in the world that you wrote about in #3?

_____

_____

5. Are there any activities or vocational or volunteer endeavors—or even relationships—you have been engaged in that were once life-giving for you, but no longer feel that way? How could you change the form of your involvement with these people or activities to create space for opportunities that are more aligned with your purpose and passions?

_____

_____

To learn more about living your purpose, I highly recommend three different books by Tama Kieves: *This Time I Dance!*, *Inspired & Unstoppable*, and *Thriving through Uncertainty*.

Edwene Gaines also gives great insights into this topic in part 4 of *The Four Spiritual Laws of Abundance*. For expert advice on navigating the falls and failures that are an inevitable part of doing new things, don't miss Brené Brown's *Rising Strong*.

EPILOGUE

April 10, 2020, marked the tenth anniversary of when I first stepped into the world as Gabrielle Elena Claiborne. In this past decade, not only have I weathered dramatic changes, but the U.S. trans landscape has also experienced seismic shifts. When I began my transition in 2010 it seemed like most Americans had very little awareness of transgender people. That began to change as trans characters started appearing regularly on popular TV shows—on *Glee* in 2012, on *Orange is the New Black* in 2013, and on *Transparent* the following year.[19]

In 2014, *Time* featured trans actress and activist Laverne Cox on its front cover with the title "Transgender Tipping Point: The Next Civil Rights Movement?" Then, in 2015, Caitlyn Jenner transitioned. More than ever before, this put transgender people in the spotlight. Talk show hosts scrambled to find gender diverse individuals to interview. Soon it felt like everyone in the world had an opinion about us—and those opinions were mixed, at best.

With the passing of North Carolina's controversial House Bill 2 and Donald Trump's election to the presidency in 2016, the political backlash began. During the next four years the Trump administration rolled back federal rights and protections for trans and gender nonconforming (TGNC) people at an alarming rate.[20] Numerous state legislative sessions have introduced and some have passed trans discriminatory legislation.

What keeps me going, in the face of all this opposition? Along with the internal lessons I've learned and shared throughout this book, there are several external factors as well. One is the knowledge that, in spite of political setbacks, the business sector recognizes the bottom line value of diversity, equity, and inclusion, so it has emerged as a strong ally for the TGNC community. Now my inclusion training and consulting firm is not just being asked to provide Trans 101 training; companies are hiring us to share best practices for organizational approaches to creating trans and nonbinary inclusive cultures, to consult with them on policy development and restroom remodels—my thirty years in the construction industry come in handy on these!—and to provide targeted trainings for managers, HR leaders, and Talent Acquisition Teams. Likewise, a broad range of organizations—from corporations to small businesses and nonprofits, from medical and mental healthcare providers to spiritual and educational institutions—are reaching out to us for trainings, consultations, and keynotes. I am even being asked to speak to various women's groups as they become more intentional about including *all* women in their equity work.

Meanwhile, I am also encouraged by statistics showing that millennials and Gen Zers are more aware of gender diversity and are themselves more gender diverse than any previous generations. Twelve percent of the millennials who responded to a 2017 Harris Poll indicated that they identify as transgender or gender nonconforming.[20] A 2018 Pew Survey showed that 35 percent of U.S. Gen Zers personally knew someone who uses gender neutral pronouns, as did one out of four millennials.[22] And this is not just a U.S. phenomenon. In a 2018 survey done by Irregular Labs—an international "Teen Vogue meets Pew" think tank—one out of four Gen Zers across the globe indicated they expect their gender identity will change at least once in their life.[23]

While these statistics are encouraging, I know the 2020 U.S. elections will have a strong impact on our national TGNC community. I hope for the best and keep working to make that happen.

Lather, Rinse, Repeat

Just as the U.S. trans landscape continues to shift, I am also seeing changes in my own life. For the past four years I have been part of another trans-affirming faith community, the Spiritual Living Center of Atlanta. One of the Center's teachings is that it is important to "own our stories but not let our stories own us." "Owning our stories" means recognizing and dealing with the impact our various life experiences have had on us. "Not letting our stories own us" means not becoming so identified with these experiences that we end up confined to seeing ourselves in just one way. This teaching is often shared in regards to the negative things we've experienced: abuse, betrayal, addiction, or illness. While one of the reasons why it is important to tell our stories is so we can work through the effects these things have had on our lives, this teaching cautions us about becoming permanently identified with our stories—which can lead to seeing ourselves as victims of our experiences. Carl Jung's quote, "I am not what has happened to me, I am what I choose to become," likewise encourages us to not get stuck in our stories.

After hearing "Own your stories, but don't let them own you" on numerous occasions, it occurred to me that this teaching could also be relevant to stories we tell about our positive experiences—things like embracing our truth and coming out as transgender, or "coming out" as an artist, a teacher, or a stay-at-home parent. While embracing the truth of my feminine essence has been the most positive thing I have ever done, lately I have realized I am so much more than trans— and so much more than my transition story. I am also an entrepreneur who loves to mentor others regarding the intricacies of owning a business. I am a TEDx and keynote speaker who enjoys motivating people to get unstuck and live authentically. I am a volunteer who likes to give of her time to make this world a better place. And I have just become a grandmother!

Owning these different facets of who I am has led me to

realize that embracing our truth is not something we do just once. Embracing our truth is an ongoing process; it is a journey, not a destination. And what our truth looks like can evolve and expand. Sometimes this expansion comes from internal nudges. Stepping more fully into our authenticity may have brought us to a place where we can gratefully say, "I love what I do!" However, in time we may hear our heart asking, "But are you doing what you love?" Anything less than a whole-hearted "Yes!" may be an invitation to take another look at what is ours to do. As I shared in the previous chapter, after I transitioned, I loved what I did as I established and grew my first three companies. But once Linda and I formed Transformation Journeys Worldwide, I realized that "doing what I loved" involved training, consulting, and giving keynotes.

Along with internal nudges, sometimes the expansion of our truth results from changing external circumstances. While being a good parent may be part of our truth, the number of hours that takes when we have young children at home is very different from the time required when our children are adults, especially if they are living on their own. Likewise, while our jobs may consume much of our time and energy, retirement can open up whole new vistas. Such changes in our life circumstances can free up time for us to explore other aspects of our authenticity.

· · ·

So now that I've shared *my* story, I want to shift our attention to *your* story. I want to ask you—wherever you are on life's journey—what beautiful facets of your ever-unfold-

153

ing truth are waiting to shine forth? What other parts of *your* authenticity are wanting to be revealed—both for your own benefit *and* for the healing of our world? To find answers to these questions, I encourage you to revisit the exercises at the end of these chapters again and again and again. When it comes to embracing *all* the facets of our truth, we must lather, rinse, repeat.

Thank you so much for reading this book and for connecting with me on the road to authenticity. Know that I wish you all the best, and I hope we have the opportunity to meet in person one day as we each continue on the life-giving, world-changing journey of embracing our truths.

Contact Gabrielle about a training or keynote at
TransformationJourneysWW.com.

ACKNOWLEDGEMENTS

The journey to authenticity is not meant to be traveled alone, and I have been blessed to have the support of so many. In addition to the individuals I mention in these chapters, there are others who have entered my life and played an integral role in my unfolding journey.

To my Atlanta Pride colleagues, thank you for intentionally making a place at the table for trans perspectives and for valuing my input as relevant to the cause. You were the first ones to give me a safe space to find and use my voice as an LGBTQ advocate.

To Sandy Mollett, Jennifer Falco, Jack Kinley, Jennifer Lutz, Dan Dunlop, Sheila Merritt, Kevin Tryner, Jeffrey Tobias Halter, Rev. Dr. David Alexander, Peter Nunn, Nzinga Shaw, Emily Schur and Lorri Palko, I am grateful to each of you for your respective life-giving contributions that have encouraged, positioned, and empowered me to show up in the world to my fullest capacity.

To all my clients, past and present (there are too many to name), thank you for being the wind beneath my wings. You've made it possible for me to learn how to run a business in a completely different gender and not only love what I do, but do what I love!

To the entire TEDxCentennialParkWomen team—especially Henna Inam, Lynn Epstein, Nancy Apatov, Charles Edwards, and Terri Deuel—thank you for recognizing the relevance of my personal story and launching me onto the biggest stage of my life—so far!

Many thanks to Lucas Miré, Gael Guzman-Medrano, David Aurilio, Teresa Wilson, Katie Herzer, Christine Cantrell, Stacey Ruth, Jill Hendrix, Lynn Epstein, Loren Reagin, and Sue Fox for reading the rough drafts of this manuscript. Your honest feedback and helpful suggestions were invaluable and have contributed greatly to the book's final form.

To the marvelous midwives who actually birthed this baby into the world—Kris Firth, copy editor extraordinaire; Darlene Carter, self-publishing guru; Kris Janovitz, photography wizard; and Lynn Epstein and Stacey Ruth, marketing marvels—many thanks for your wisdom, patience, and support. And to Jack Kinley, incredibly creative cover designer, eternal gratitude for expertly conveying the essence of my work in a visual format.

To my family, I'll be the first to acknowledge that this

journey hasn't been easy. . . for any of us. Know that I am eternally grateful for each of you who have found ways, however large or small, to move forward with me, redefining and courageously navigating what our relationships can look like now. You will never know just how much that has meant— and continues to mean—to me. I am also grateful for each of you who are still grappling with this aspect of my authenticity. Please know that I cherish all we have shared to this point and I look forward to that day when we can sit down together, face to face, and get reacquainted. I love ALL of you so much.

To Linda Herzer—my best friend, business partner, and the one who reminds me daily, "You're gonna be okay"—my deepest gratitude for so beautifully capturing and articulating the width, breadth, and depth of my journey of embracing the gender aspect of my truth. Your willingness to listen, grieve, understand, grapple with, laugh, and even push back as we co-created this book has invited me, as Brené Brown would say, to step into the arena even more vulnerably and courageously than I ever have before. Thanks to your unwavering commitment, I can joyfully and gratefully say, "This book truly reflects my lived experience."

APPENDIX
Understanding Transgender People

Here is the most important thing you need to know in order to understand transgender people: all human beings have something that determines their gender. Contrary to popular opinion, it is not their anatomy. What medical and mental health experts know is that every human being's gender is determined by their gender identity, that is, by their internal knowing of their gender.

The vast majority of people have the privilege of having a gender identity that matches the gender they were assigned at birth—a gender assignment that, quite frankly, was based on anatomy. These people are cisgender. But a small percentage of individuals throughout the world (in the United States, best estimates range from .6 percent to 1.8 percent) have a gender identity that does not match the gender we were assigned at birth.[24] The umbrella term transgender describes us. (Note: the word transgender is most respectfully used as an adjective, so please don't refer to us as transgenders or as being transgendered.)

There are many gender identities under the transgender umbrella. Those like myself who were raised as boys, but who resonate with the feminine, are trans women. Those who were assigned female at birth, but know themselves to be male, are trans men. People who do not resonate with either male or female, nor with any gender, are agender. Individuals who know themselves to be a combination of genders identify as nonbinary, genderqueer, gender fluid, bigender, or as some other gender, depending on the particular combination of genders they experience. (You can find definitions of these various terms on the Human Rights Campaign website at https://hrc.org/resources/glossary-of-terms.)

The reality that some people have gender identities that differ from their biological sex should come as no surprise, since medical experts know that a fetus's brain and reproductive organs begin developing about four weeks apart in utero.[25] Given this developmental time lag, it's not hard to imagine that a baby's grey matter and their genitalia might receive different messaging about their gender.

But exactly what causes a person to have a gender identity that does not match the gender they were assigned at birth is still unknown. For many years, researchers assumed this difference in the human experience must result from a mental disorder, so they researched psychological causes.

However, years of research and the evidence from decades of therapy sessions conducted by mental health experts have led both the American Psychological Association and the World Health Organization to determine that being transgender is not a mental disorder—it is simply another facet of the diverse human experience. These determinations have led researchers to begin focusing their experiments on the biological causes of gender identity. While the various approaches to this biological research have suggested possible theories, conclusive evidence has yet to emerge.

Nevertheless, researchers have learned that gender is a whole lot more complex than Western culture leads us to believe. Even biological sex is not cut and dry! Medical professionals know that there are many intersex people—those for whom the biological components of sex, that is, internal and external reproductive organs and chromosome patterns, are present in ways that are not strictly male or female. For example, females have XX chromosomes, ovaries, and vaginas. But some intersex people have XX chromosomes, ovaries, and penises. Likewise, males have XY chromosomes, testes, and penises. But some intersex people have XY chromosomes, testes, and vaginas. In fact, there are more than a dozen different combinations of reproductive organs and chromosome patterns that can result in someone being intersex; these are just two examples. While it is hard to determine exactly how many people are intersex, best estimates are that intersex people are as common as redheads.

Knowledge of this diversity within biological sex, coupled

with growing awareness of the diversity of gender identities, has prompted many countries and a growing number of U.S. states to legally recognize the complexity of gender. Across the globe, more than a dozen countries offer a third gender option on passports or allow their citizens to self-declare their gender on legal documents.[26] In the United States, at least nineteen states and the District of Columbia offer gender markers of M, F, or X on drivers licenses, in recognition of their male, female, and intersex or gender diverse residents.[27]

As I share in my Trans 101 training, along with gender identity and biological sex, there are two other aspects of gender: gender expression and sexual orientation. Gender expression has to do with how we express or present our gender on the outside, through our hair styles, the clothing we wear, and our accessories. Mannerisms and vocal registers are other key components of gender expression. Sexual orientation has to do with whom we are attracted to physically and romantically. On the internet you can find helpful diagrams like the Genderbread Person and the Gender Unicorn that show how each of these aspects of gender exist on continuums. What unites us as human beings is the fact that we all have these four aspects of gender. What makes each of us unique is where any one of us falls on any one of these four very different continuums.

And while we're on the topic of the four aspects of gender, let's address a common misperception. The acronym LGBT leads many to believe that being lesbian, gay, or bisexual is the same thing as being transgender. But being L, G, or B has to do with one's sexual orientation, while being T is all about, and only about, one's gender identity. And in the same way that a cisgender person might be gay, straight, or bi, or have any one of the many other sexual orientations that people experience, transgender people can also be gay, straight, bi, etc.

While there is much that can be learned about transgender people, what I have shared here provides you with at least a basic understanding. If you would like to learn more, please see the articles and videos linked off the Resources page of my company's website at https://transformationjourneysww.com/.

NOTES

Chapter 1

1. S. E. James, J. L. Herman, S. Rankin, M. Keisling, L. Mottet, and M. Anafi, *The Report of the 2015 U.S. Transgender Survey*, Washington, DC: National Center for Transgender Equality, 2016, https://transequality.org/sites/default/files/docs/USTS-Full-Report-FINAL.PDF.

2. Jaime M. Grant, Lisa A. Mottet, Justin Tanis, Jack Harrison, Jody L. Herman, and Mara Keisling, *Injustice at Every Turn: A Report of the National Transgender Discrimination Survey*, Washington, DC: National Center for Transgender Equality and National Gay and Lesbian Task Force, 2011, https://www.transequality.org/sites/default/files/docs/resources/NTDS_Report.pdf.

NOTES

Chapter 2

3. R. Travers, G. Bauer, J. Pyne, and K. Bradley for the Trans PULSE Project; L. Gale and M. Papadimitriou, *Impacts of Strong Parental Support for Trans Youth: A Report Prepared for Children's Aid Society of Toronto and Delisle Youth Services,* 2 October 2012, http://transpulseproject.ca/research/impacts-of-strong-parental-support-for-trans-youth/.

Chapter 3

4. James, et al., *Report of the 2015 U.S. Transgender Survey.*

5. Edwene Gaines, *The Four Spiritual Laws of Prosperity* (New York: Rodale Books, 2005), 96.

6. Ibid., 84..

Chapter 4

7. Ibid., 119–120, 124 (italics are mine).

8. Brené Brown, *Daring Greatly*, (New York: Avery, 2012), 71.

9. Ibid., 67.

10. Chuck Lorre, Eddie Gorodetsky, and Gemma Baker, *Mom,* American CBS sitcom, pilot episode, dir. Pamela Fryman, September 13, 2013, https://en.wikipedia.org/wiki/Mom_(season_1). Any quoted material from *Mom* is from my best memory, not a transcript.

11. Ibid., season 7, "Higgledy-Piggledy and a Cat Show," dir. James Widdoes, December 19, 2019, https://en.wikipedia.org/wiki/Mom_(season_7).

12. Ibid.

Chapter 5

13. Brené Brown, *Rising Strong: How the Ability to Reset Transforms the Way We Live, Love, Parent, and Lead* (New York: Random House, 2015), 146.

14. Ibid., 146.

Chapter 7

15. Travers et al., *Impacts of Strong Parental Support for Trans Youth.*

16. Gaines, *The Four Spiritual Laws of Prosperity*, 196.

17. Tama Kieves, *Thriving through Uncertainty* (New York: TarcherPerigree, 2018), 163.

18. Ibid., 4.

Epilogue

19. See "Alex Newell," https://en.wikipedia.org/wiki/Alex_Newell; "Orange Is the New Black," https://en.wikipedia.org/wiki/Orange_Is_the_New_Black;and "Transparent (2014–2019) Full Cast & Crew," https://www.imdb.com/title/tt3502262/fullcredits.

20. The National Center for Transgender Equality lists the Trump administration's record of action—changes implemented or attempted—against transgender people on the NCTE website: "The Discrimination Administration," https://transequality.org/the-discrimination-administration.

21. GLAAD, "Accelerating Acceptance 2017: A Harris

Poll survey of Americans' acceptance of LGBTQ people," https://www.glaad.org/files/aa/2017_GLAAD_Accelerating_ Acceptance.pdf.

22. In Pew Research Center, "Generation Z Looks a Lot Like Millennials on Key Social and Political Issues," https:// www.pewsocialtrends.org/2019/01/17/generation-z-looks-a-lot-like-millennials-on-key-social-and-political-issues/.

23. In "The Irregular Report #2: Fluidity," https://www. irregularlabs.com/pages/shop#irregular-reports-section.

Appendix

24. Per UCLA Williams School of Law, "How Many Adults Identify as Transgender in the United States?" https://williamsinstitute.law.ucla.edu/publications/trans-adults-united-states/ (.6%), and M.M. Johns, R. Lowry, J. Andrzejewski, et al., "Transgender Identity and Experiences of Violence Victimization, Substance Use, Suicide Risk, and Sexual Risk Behaviors Among High School Students—19 States and Large Urban School Districts, 2017," MMWR Morb. Mort. Wkly Rep. 2019; 68:67–71, https://www.cdc. gov/mmwr/volumes/68/wr/mm6803a3.htm (1.8%).

25. Mayo Clinic, "Pregnancy Week by Week," https:// www.mayoclinic.org/healthy-lifestyle/pregnancy-week-by-week/in-depth/prenatal-care/art-20045302.

26. Wikipedia entry, "Legal recognition on non-binary gender," https://en.wikipedia.org/wiki/Legal_recognition_of_ non-binary_gender#United_Kingdom.

27. Movement Advancement Project (MAP), "Identity

Document Laws and Policies," https://www.lgbtmap.org/ equality-maps/identity_document_laws.

GLOSSARY

Cisgender—Adjective describing people whose gender identity matches the sex/gender they were assigned at birth.

Gender diverse—An umbrella term including people whose gender identity or gender expression differs from stereotypical male/female cultural expectations. See "transgender" and "nonbinary."

Gender expression—The manner in which a person expresses or presents their gender to others. Elements of a person's gender expression include clothing, hairstyles, mannerisms, vocal register, etc.

Gender identity—A person's deeply held sense of their own gender. One's gender identity can be the same as or different from the sex/gender they were assigned at birth.

GLOSSARY

Gender marker—The "M" for male, "F" for female, "X" for other, or "U" for unspecified that appears on legal documents.

LGBTQ—acronym for lesbian, gay, bisexual, transgender, queer.

Nonbinary—An umbrella term including persons who identify as neither male nor female, or as some combination of both.

Transgender—An adjective that can be used in a specific sense or as an umbrella term for people whose gender identities do not match the sex/gender they were assigned at birth.

It is used specifically to indicate trans men (people assigned female at birth who identify as male) or trans women (people assigned male at birth who identity as female).

As an umbrella term, it also includes other people whose gender identities do not match the sex/gender they were assigned at birth, such as nonbinary, agender, gender fluid, genderqueer and bigender persons, etc.

Note: *Trans* is a respectful term that is short for *transgender.* It is disrespectful to use *transgender* as a noun (*transgenders*), adverb (*transgendered*) or as a movement (*transgenderism).*

Transition—The process in which a person goes from living as one gender to living as a different gender. Each person's transition process is unique and may or may not include social, legal, or physicals aspects.

RECOMENDED READING

Books to Support You as
You Embrace Your Truth

Brown, Brené. *Daring Greatly: How the Courage to Be Vulnerable Transforms the Way We Live, Love, Parent, and Lead.* New York: Avery, 2012.

————. *Rising Strong: How the Ability to Reset Transforms the Way We Live, Love, Parent, and Lead.* New York: Random House, 2015.

Gaines, Edwene. *The Four Spiritual Laws of Prosperity: A Simple Guide to Unlimited Abundance.* New York: Rodale Books, 2005.

Hay, Louise. *You Can Heal Your Life.* Carlsbad, CA: Hay House, 1987.

Herzer, Linda Tatro. *The Bible and the Transgender Experience: How Scripture Supports Gender Variance.* Cleveland: Pilgrim Press, 2016.

Kieves, Tama. *Inspired & Unstoppable: Wildly Succeeding in Your Life's Work.* New York: Tarcher/Penguin, 2013.

———. *This Time I Dance! Creating the Work You Love.* New York: Tarcher/Penguin, 2006.

———. *Thriving through Uncertainty: Moving Beyond Fear of the Unknown and Making Change Work for You.* New York: TarcherPerigree, 2018.

Reeves, Paula. *Heart Sense: Unlocking Your Highest Purpose and Deepest Desires.* York Beach, ME: Conari Press, 2003.

Ruiz, Don Miguel. *The Four Agreements: A Practical Guide to Personal Freedom.* San Rafael, CA: Amber-Allen Publishing, 1997.

Williamson, Marianne. *A Woman's Worth.* New York: Random House, 1993.

Coming Out Resources for LGBTQ People and Their Loved Ones

For coming out resources for persons of various gender identities, sexual orientations, ethnicities, and religions, see a wide selection of guides created by the Human Rights Campaign (HRC) at https://www.hrc.org/resources/coming-out.

Resources for teens and young adults include the following: https://www.thetrevorproject.org/trvr_support_center/ coming-out/ and https://www.glsen.org/activity/coming-out-resource-lgbtq-students.

PFLAG provides support for LGBTQ individuals and their loved ones. Resources specifically for loved ones can be found at https://pflag.org/Family.

PFLAG's resource for supporting the loved ones of transgender individuals can be found at https://pflag.org/Family.

A Resource for Learning More About Transgender People

On the Resources page of my company website there are links to sites where you can learn more about transgender and non-binary children, youth, and adults; gender-related terms and definitions; and how to interact respectfully with gender diverse people: https://transformationjourneysww.com/resources/.

ABOUT THE AUTHOR

Gabrielle Claiborne is a TEDx and keynote speaker, dynamic trainer, successful entrepreneur, and recognized community leader whose work has been featured in *Forbes* and on NPR. She is the CEO and co-founder of Transformation Journeys Worldwide, a training and consulting firm dedicated to helping organizations create fully trans and nonbinary inclusive cultures.

Gabrielle has been honored as Atlanta's Best Trans Activist, Emory University's Pride Alum of the Year, the Georgia Division of the U.S. Small Business Administration's LGBT Small Business Champion, and the *Atlanta Business Chronicle's* Outstanding Voice for Diversity and Inclusion. Her firm has been recognized as a recipient of the Atlanta Hawk's True Comes in All Colors Award and the OUT Georgia

Business Alliance's Small Business of the Year.

For five years Gabrielle served on the Atlanta Pride Board of Directors. She currently sits on the City of Atlanta's Mayoral LGBTQ Advisory Board and the National LGBT Chamber of Commerce's TGNC Inclusion Task Force. She serves as the Board Secretary and Inclusion Chair for the OUT Georgia Business Alliance. A lifelong church leader, Gabrielle was elected to the Executive Board at City of Light Atlanta, directed their choir, and founded and led the church's trans support group.

She is the proud parent of three adult children and one Bengal kitty and the delighted grandparent of one new grandbaby. Gabrielle lives in Atlanta, Georgia.

TransformationJourneysWW.com

LinkedIn.com/IN/Gabrielle-Claiborne

Facebook.com/TransformationJourneysWW

Instagram.com/TransformationJourneysW

Twitter.com/TransformJourny

CPSIA information can be obtained
at www.ICGtesting.com
Printed in the USA
LVHW041044150920
666055LV00004B/360